Seven
American
Catholics

Seven
American
Catholics

by
John
Deedy

THE THOMAS MORE PRESS
Chicago, Illinois

ISBN 0-88347-087-X

The chapters on Leonard Feeney, Cardinal O'Connell and Cardinal Spellman originally appeared, in slightly different form, in *The Critic,* and are printed here by permission.

CONTENTS

For my "big sisters,"
Lou, Beth, Mae

FOREWORD

It might seem that any unifying thread in my choice of the seven persons who are the subject of this book is a tenuous one. Most of my subjects have nothing in common except their religion and their nationality. *Except!* Having religion and nationality in common, in a sense they have everything in common. Moreover, being important in their respective fields, at their respective times, each at one point or another has touched the lives of us all. Some still do, as a matter of fact—although at the time of the writing of this book only two were still living, and one of them has since died: Father Leonard Feeney.

Not all of the seven persons under discussion here are favorites of mine. But each has fascinated me for one reason or another, and each has had an influence on me, however obliquely. For instance, Cardinal O'Connell and I were generations removed from one another, and removed also by miles; he reigned (quite literally) in Boston, while I was a mere diocesan, layman to boot, of the old Diocese of Springfield. Yet my growing up Catholic in the ecclesiastical Province of New England brought me quite directly under his influence and that of his episcopal legacy. Similarly, growing up Catholic in twentieth-century America meant that I could not escape, for a time at least, a political inheritance from Al Smith, although I was not old enough to vote for him when he stood for the presidency—the first Catholic to be a candidate of a major American political party for the highest office in the land. That was 1928. I was five years old.

My reservations show in my treatment of my subjects. But I have sought to be fair to all, including O'Connell . . . including Smith, who probably ranks as the most disappointing of my seven—for me personally. Indeed, fairness was the easiest part of my task. Few lives are such total losses that one cannot find redeeming qualities in the persons leading them. Be it said now: None of my subjects is considered by me to be a total loss, even the more mischievous of them like Leonard Feeney, who, if nothing else, held himself open to reconciliation with the church of his ordination.

If I wear my heart on my sleeve in any of these essays, it is in that dealing with Dorothy Day. I make no apologies for the fact. I am not an intimate of Dorothy's; I am not an alumnus of the Catholic Worker movement. But I have been close enough to her and to the movement to know that she is genuine, that she is no manufactured hero, no neat product of a slick public-relations operation. In point of fact, if Dorothy Day had Dr. Tom Dooley's public-relations instincts, his facility for getting the last inch of publicity out of every word and deed, well then, the Nobel Prize—if that is the highest humanitarian award to which any of us might aspire—would long since have been hers.

In arriving at my seven subjects, I eliminated seven-times-seven. I considered, for example, Phil Murray, the labor leader who was so prominent in the formation of the Congress of Industrial Organizations (CIO) and in the fight against Communists in the labor movement around 1949-1950. I considered, more currently, Dan Berrigan and his brother and sister-in-law, Phil Berrigan and Elizabeth McAlister, the anti-war activists of the Vietnam national nightmare. I considered even Vince Lombardi, the guy who helped "jockify" America and who helped make professional football into the great American Sunday ritual for at least part of the year—what church was when I was a boy. I settled on my seven, not because they were more important, singly or collectively, than those I eliminated, but because, with the possible exception of the Berrigans, they entered more directly into my thought and being. Also because, unlike the Berrigans, to mention them again, they were sufficiently removed in time and events to allow for more conclusive, less partisan treatment, pro or con. Thus Leonard Feeney. He was aged, the course virtually run, when I sat down to write about him. If he had been in his middle years, I probably would not have touched him, for he would then have been still very much in transit—much as the Berrigans are yet, I feel.

My seven are not offered as giants in the historical sense of, say, a Winston Churchill or a Pope John XXIII—although I am willing to be proved wrong by history in any case it may choose. But giant or not, each was significant for better or for worse in some special way, and each leaves a footstep or two, however faint, on the sands of time. I've attempted to outline them. If I have missed some, blame it on the fact that sands can shift with each new stirring of the breeze.

Many people assisted me in the writing of this book, giving generously of their time for interviews and answering long and sometimes impatient letters of inquiry from me. Several of my sources requested anonymity, particularly in connection with the chapter on Cardinal Spellman; obviously some believe that the long arm can reach out yet from that grave. Because of these requests, I have decided against ticking off names in a long list of acknowledgements. I elect instead to speak an unspecific thank you to all who helped. They know who they are, and I want each to know that I am grateful.

Some sources had no qualms, of course, about being identified, and they are quoted in the text. I'll let the reader discover them in the reading of the book.

J.D.

New York, 1977

I

ALFRED E. SMITH

The Happy Warrior Who Was Really Sad

I GREW UP in a house where you were quiet when Father Coughlin was on the radio, and where you spoke reverentially, always, about Al Smith. Not that Al Smith was a priest or some other impeccable exemplar on which to model your life, although Lord knows he was so esteemed by many Irish Catholics. Al Smith was a politician, but he was different from most other Irish-Catholic politicians, who stood to be libeled in the breath next to that in which they were lauded. Al Smith was different because he confirmed for individual Irish Catholics so much of what Father Coughlin was raging against from Royal Oak: the conspiracy in the land. Father Coughlin saw this conspiracy in terms of socialists and Jews. In Al Smith's lot, Irish Catholics saw this conspiracy in terms of their traditional *bête noire*, Protestants. Al Smith was living demonstration that the United States was a Protestant preserve, and that the Irish Catholic place was away at the fringe. In the 1920s, they weren't entirely wrong in their assumptions. Protestants indeed did still enjoy the ascendancy, and Catholics— particularly Irish Catholics, because they were here first and in greatest numbers—were the objects, if not of official religious discrimination, then of a barely cloaked religious bias that was organized and personal. That bias combined with other factors to cost Al Smith the presidency of the United States.

Irish Catholics were bitter about that turn of events. How well I remember the hurt feelings carried for years by senior kin, grandparents and parents, uncles and aunts. But hurt though they and their generations were, there was still something curiously consoling for them about Al Smith's fate. It wasn't a case, once again, of the Irish taking satisfaction in the failure of one of their own. Nor were they being masochistic, although social masochism can be a penchant of American Catholics. There was consolation because Al Smith's fate confirmed deep Irish-Catholic suspicions about Protestant America—and, in the process, fortified them as a people. The Lord promised discrimination; he promised Catholics, didn't he, that they would be despised for the baptism that was theirs. In Al Smith, wasn't the word made true? What I'm saying is that there's a certain pride that comes with being the object of religious prejudice, a strength from being singled out and set apart—provided, that is, that there is no secret inner shame or doubt about the faith that brings this on. In other words, just as an elitism motivates the discriminator, there is, or can be, an elitism in being the object of discrimination. The badge of shame/honor syndrome. In the instance of the person discriminated against, this elitism can quicken the spirit, fortify the subculture.

In so far as Catholics, and American Irish Catholics in particular, interpreted Al Smith's presidential defeat as an application of Protestant religious prejudice, both spirit and subculture were strengthened. Catholics were made unmistakably aware that they were different, and pride and confidence quickened in many because of this difference. So it was that for three decades more subculture and faith flourished; adversity produced its frequent effect. The question is whether it was accident or inevitability that both— church and subculture—should have begun to come apart once a Catholic had made it all the way to the top, routing the vestiges of religious political prejudice in the process and leaving a people and a religion with no blatant opposition to spur them onward, to confirm culture within a culture, their special religious status, or lack thereof, within an officially religious albeit Protestant society. Put another way, are those folks nutty who argue that it would have been better for subculture and faith had a Catholic never been elected to the White House?

Nutty I believe they are, although theirs is a question never to be conclusively answered. For it's the stuff of barroom chatter. Was Lou Gehrig better in the clutch than Reggie Jackson? Were the Yankees of 1927 better than those of 1977? You never settle questions like those, just as you don't settle questions about the break-up of the Catholic subculture and religious unity by fingering the success of John Fitzgerald Kennedy. If the proposition isn't crazy to begin with, there are other crucial factors omitted from the cause/effect equation. Like the coming apart of the Catholic faith throughout the wider world, at least in its institutional embodiment.

But whatever may be said about the Kennedy triumph of 1960, this can be said of the Smith defeat of 1928: It really did feed the Irish Catholic psyche; it helped the American Irish Catholic subculture survive another thirty years; and it probably made easier the Kennedy run for the presidency. If nothing else, the Kennedy candidacy was not saddled with any residue of resentment against Catholics as a class because of the economic disaster that followed the election of 1928. So real had been the religious prejudice against Catholics in 1928 that it is not inconceivable that some legacy of bitterness would have attached to Kennedy or whoever the first Catholic was who attempted to succeed where Smith had failed. No one entering the White House in 1929 was likely to have been able to head off the stock-market crash of that year and forestall the Great Depression of the 1930s. The economic forces were too far advanced towards disaster. Had Al Smith won the presidency, an historical onus would have been his, and the brushes that are reserved for the tarring of Herbert Hoover's memory would assuredly have been applied, by whatever twisted logic, to him and to the first latter-day Al Smith who came along, John Fitzgerald Kennedy. Thus the paradox of history, that in losing, Al Smith was spared a darker historical fate. And Jack Kennedy was spared some heavy luggage in the bargain.

Al Smith was born Alfred Emanuel Smith on December 30, 1873, on New York City's Lower East Side. His mother was a Mulvehill, one generation removed from Ireland; his father was a native American, a widower, fifteen years older than his second wife, and of obscure ancestry. This obscurity led many to suggest that Al Smith was not *all* Irish; a pox on *their* house. But Al Smith certainly *lived* all Irish. He grew up in an Irish enclave, associated with Irishers throughout his youth; he married a Dunn, and minded carefully the Irish priests who ran the block. He went to St. James Parochial School, served at the altar in the church next door, and displayed a flair for theatrics and oratory. Young Al could have been headed for the New York City Fire Department or a clerkship in a business office, but his father died when he was 12, and two years later, a month before completing the eighth grade, he was forced to drop out of school to help the family make ends meet. The father, a truck-wagon driver, had left nothing; the mother was doing piece-work in an umbrella factory. Mary, Al's sister, was two years younger than he and, of course, too young to go yet into the world. He would put food on the table and help pay the rent.

Al Smith worked at a succession of jobs: errand boy for a trucker (for which he was paid the grand sum of $3 a week), clerk in a wholesale commission house at the Fulton Fish Market, a boiler worker. Beyond St. James, there was no formal education, although he would retort one day to a fellow Assemblyman in Albany that he owned a degree, an F.F.M. "I don't believe I've heard of such a degree," said the querulous Assemblyman. "Fulton Fish Market," Smith shot back.

In quite a literal sense, Fulton Fish Market was Smith's campus. So were the sidewalks of New York, East Side, West Side, all around the town. He carried New York's coarse accent—carried it as proudly as the cigar in his mouth and the brown derby that he plunked on his head as a young man and seemingly never removed. His imagination was fed by such wonders as the new Brooklyn Bridge, within whose extending shadow he slept at night; his awe, by such New York phenomena as the blizzard of 1888; his smarts, by foamy conversations at Irish saloons. (The noble experiment had not yet begun.) Al Smith's world grew, but it never outgrew his F.F.M. Fulton's Fish Market gave his tongue a salty wit with which to classify friend or foe, mostly the latter. An adversary had "an eye as glassy as a dead cod's," or a handshake "like a frozen mackerel." A trying situation would be summed up in a sea phrase, with the help of a mixed metaphor. Of a fistful of confusing legislative bills, junior Assemblyman Smith would explain that he could "tell a haddock from a hake by the look in its eye," but he couldn't tell those bills "from a bale of hay."

Al Smith went to Albany as a man of Tammany Hall, the notorious political organization that originated in 1789 as the Society of St. Tammany, a fraternal aid association. Tammany identified with the national Democratic Party, and in time came to control Democratic politics in New York City, lock, stock and payoff bag. But Tammany wasn't all bad. If

it was corrupt enough to produce a "Boss" Tweed in
the nineteenth century, it was solid enough to produce
an Al Smith in the twentieth. But whereas Tammany
Hall would raise Al Smith up, it would also help undo
him by rendering him in many eyes suspect by association. Some isolated incidents notwithstanding, Al
Smith was never a tool of Tammany; but as its
creature he was viewed warily in many parts of the
country when he made his unsuccessful move to shift
his political base from Albany to Washington. That's
when Tammany hurt him. The irony—only one of
many in Smith's life—is that he did more than any
other New York political figure of his time to
neutralize the influence of the machine in city and
state politics.

Al Smith's entry into politics was both instinctual
and fortuitous. He might have preferred a theatrical
career, but the theater had a slightly disreputable aura
about it—at least it did to the Dunns, whose daughter,
Catherine, Al aspired to marry. And what could have
been more honorable for a nice young Catholic boy of
Irish background, next to the holy priesthood, than a
career in politics? Al Smith debuted as a speechifier
for an anti-Tammany congressional candidate. The
candidate lost and the experience taught Al Smith his
first political lesson: You don't fight the organization;
party regularity is the key to political success. Irony
number 2: Smith would live by the principle of party
regularity, but late in his career, after his political
leadership had waned and Franklin Delano Roose-

velt's had taken over, he would abandon regularity, support Alf Landon and Wendell Willkie, and make a bloody ass of himself.

In his fledgling days Smith was an habitué of Tom Foley's saloon at Oliver and Water Streets. Saloons were the minor league clubs, as it were, of Tammany Hall, the places where new talent was ferreted out and where given its testing. Saloon owners were often politicians themselves, minor office holders, political appointees, district leaders, spotters. Foley fit the category, and his eye fell early on Al Smith. Smith was put out stumping, rewarded with an $800-a-year job as process server for the commissioner of jurors, and finally in 1903 was handed the Democratic nomination as Tammany's candidate for Second Assembly District seat, a gesture that was tantamount to election. He had made the jump to the Big Leagues. On the first Tuesday in January, 1904, Al Smith climbed aboard a train for Albany and embarked on a political career that would fall just short of the ultimate success.

In Albany, Al Smith was a quick learner. Like other hand-picked Tammany politicos, he was expected to vote as he was told. Consequently Al was regarded indifferently by his seniors in the Assembly. He was bent on independence, however. And determined to make his mark, he set about mastering the intricacies of Assembly politics. He did this quietly and inconspicuously, dutifully doing his homework in some flea-bag hotel or modest rooming house, and, almost while heads were turned, becoming the most proficient of legislators, a man who knew the system better than the most veteran of legislators. More importantly, he had a keen eye for the crucial social issues, and the last thing in his mind was partisan, political advantage. There was nothing cynical about Al Smith. He felt social wrongs deeply and acted on them out of sincere, genuine interest. There was no problem with Tammany about this. To its surprise it discovered that the common good was Tammany's good also. It could replace the Christmas gift basket with something much more meaningful and enduring: solid social legislation. Hooray for Al!

Al Smith's success in Albany and his emergence as a figure of national significance rested largely on two services: his work as a member of the Assembly's Cities Committee, which revised the New York City Charter; and his vice-chairmanship of the special Factory Commission, which came into existence after the shocking Triangle Shirtwaist Company fire of 1911, a blaze that claimed 146 lives and brought the sweatshop in America at last under public scrutiny. In the first instance, Al Smith did the educating: floor debate on the New York City Charter revealed him as a quick, informed defender of home rule and of the rights of the anonymous taxpayer. The performance was stunning. In the second, he was the educated. The Triangle Shirtwaist probe broadened to factories generally in the state and extended over four years. Through investigations, hearings, and reports, Smith was exposed to some of the more advanced social thinkers and activists of the day, including Samuel

21

Gompers of the American Federation of Labor; Frances Perkins, a future Secretary of Labor in the Roosevelt Administration; Dr. Henry Moskowitz of the Ethical Culture Society; Belle Israel, the future Mrs. Moskowitz, a member of the staff of Educational Alliance. The Triangle Shirtwaist probe was a challenge to old concepts, a prod to new ideas (including women's suffrage, eventually), and out of it were to come a host of recommendations in the areas of worker sanitation, health and fire-safety, wages and work-day conditions covering women and children, and workmen's compensation benefits. The recommendations were speedily translated into law, much of the legislation originating in the Assembly with Smith. He bulldozed bills through committee, argued their validity on the floor, fought off the vested commercial interests, corralled necessary votes, and in effect provided the nation with a first glimpse of the New Deal that would be bequeathed to the land a quarter-century later . . . not by him, however, but by a one-time Albany colleague, the "Frank" of the "Dear Al, Dear Frank" correspondence, Franklin Delano Roosevelt. Thus irony number 3: that Al Smith would one day break with Roosevelt, and in renouncing him renounce tremendous personal and professional social values of his own—almost everything, in fact, that he stood for politically.

His work in the Assembly propelled Al Smith upwards with Tammany and in the Democratic Party. He was tapped for sheriff of New York City, a post not so exalted as lucrative. It was worth more than $60,000 annually in fees and made no great demands on the officeholder. Al Smith welcomed the money for the uptown affluence it made available to a downtown family. Next, he was boomed for mayor of New York City, but in 1917 Tammany had someone else to take care of and Smith settled for nomination for president of the Board of Aldermen, winning the seat easily and winning points with the chieftains at the same time for his agreeableness. It was a virtue that paid off. In 1918, Al Smith got his shot at the governorship, and though it was a Republican year, he edged in by a margin of 15,000 votes. A bigger surprise, and a blessing for Al Smith, was that the Tammany leadership did not encumber the new governor with obligations and demands. As Robert Moses was to word it years later, "There were no monkeys pinned to Governor Smith's back. He traveled light and less encumbered than any Ark-of-the-Covenant Republican upstater of his day."

Al Smith served four terms as governor. It might have been five, except he lost in 1920, the year of the Harding-Coolidge sweep. He could console himself, however, that in the State of New York he ran more than a million votes ahead of the national Democratic ticket of Cox and Roosevelt. Smith marked time for two years as the $50,000-a-year chairman of the board of United States Trucking Corporation (Al Smith was not one to disdain lush opportunities), then he was back on the ballot for governor in 1922, 1924, 1926, and was victorious each time.

No question but that he won on his record. The *New*

Republic, even before his first term was completed, was calling Smith "one of the ablest governors" the state ever had. And the *Dictionary of American Biography* was to credit him with playing "an almost classic progressive role" in a decade little known for reform politics. He pressed for the 48-hour week at a time when employers could demand almost any hourly commitment from workers. He streamlined state government, reducing some one hundred and fifty-two overlapping agencies to a manageable number of cabinet-level positions; he reduced taxes, improved parks and recreational facilities, promoted low-cost housing, advanced welfare benefits, expanded educational systems and launched the first broadly conceived mental-health program in the country. Though unsuccessful in extending public control over the development of waterway and water-power resources, he did manage to block efforts in 1922 and 1927 to transfer many prime sites to private, narrow interests —strategic accomplishments that one day made possible at less cost the state's vast hydroelectric system. Al Smith's Power Authority Act was blocked by Republican legislative majorities, but Franklin Roosevelt as governor made it one of his priorities, and in 1931 a measure similar to Smith's did pass. Republican Governor Tom Dewey went on to enlarge the program in 1954.

As these events transpired, Al Smith built a solid reputation as a civil libertarian, although it is doubtful that this achievement counted much at the grassroots. The feelings of the day were intense towards radicals of any sort, and were being constantly fanned by William Randolph Hearst, a Smith-baiter all his life, and his chain of Hearst newspapers. Al Smith vetoed several anti-sedition measures, and spoke up for five duly elected Socialist Assemblymen who were expelled by the Assembly. Smith denounced the action as a discreditable piece of counterextremism. Hearst seethed. In another celebrated instance, he pardoned an Irish revolutionary, declaring that "public assertion of an erroneous doctrine" was insufficient grounds for detaining anyone. Then, by way of demonstrating that that pardon was no partisan thing, he extended clemency to a Communist prisoner because he posed "no clear and present danger" to the state. When it came to the Ku Klux Klan, however, Smith willingly signed a bill virtually outlawing the KKK in the state—a piece of ideological inconsistency, perhaps, but an anticipatory backhand to an organization that caused him many a headache when he ran for the presidency. The populists were not enthused.

When governor, as throughout his life, Al Smith's religion was a decisive influence on thought and action. He was, by way of comparison to John Kennedy, a formal, knee-jerk Catholic, which Kennedy never was. But Al Smith possessed the same Kennedy quality of independence from clerical dominance and the same Kennedy sensitivity to the separation clause of the Constitution. Thus, when an emissary came from Cardinal O'Connell of Boston in 1924 urging opposition to a child-labor bill, Smith made it clear that he would heed the Church's authority on faith and morals, but on matters of economic, social and political concern he was his own man, and ever would be. Al Smith would spell out his Catholicism publicly and precisely a few years later when his religion was cited in a famous *Atlantic Monthly* article as an obstacle to his election as President, although the explication was less Smith's than it was that of Father Francis P. Duffy of "Fighting 69th" World War I fame. It was stilted and stiff, most uncharacteristic of anything from Al Smith. Smith's strength lay in the immediate gut reaction to a challenge, and if he had stuck to instinct he might have handled the religion problem much more persuasively. In a word, he would have been much better off to have stuck with his immediate response to the highly legalistic *Atlantic Monthly* piece: ". . . I never heard of these encyclicals and bulls and books that the *Atlantic* author writes about. They have nothing to do with being a Catholic." Instead he was talked into the formal reply, and though that reply was an antecedent to John F. Kennedy's reply to a similar challenge years later in Houston, Smith's had none of the finesse of Kennedy's. The specter of creeping Catholicism would not be laid to rest until September 12, 1960.

Al Smith's bid for the presidency began tentatively in 1920, when his name was placed in nomination at the Democratic National Convention in San Francisco by W. Bourke Cochran, like Smith a product of Rome and of Tammany, an orator of the "silver tongue." It was a favorite-son nomination, and predictably it achieved nothing except to dramatize Smith's availability and his long hope. In 1924, in a convention held at the old Madison Square Garden in New York City, the Smith chips were all on the table, but the convention deadlocked through one hundred ballots between him and William Gibbs McAdoo, a native Georgian, corporation lawyer, Woodrow Wilson's son-in-law and manufactured populist in the image of William Jennings Bryan. McAdoo was what Smith was not on two of the most important concerns for a conservative and still essentially rural America: he was Protestant and he was Prohibitionist. If national conventions nominated on simple majority, the 1924 nomination would have been McAdoo's. He led Smith ballot after ballot—431½ to 241, 495 to 331½. Smith, in fact, never received more than 368 delegate votes; McAdoo went as high as 530. Early in the balloting, it was as obvious as the old Third Avenue el that Smith would never get the nomination, but he stubbornly refused to withdraw, and insisted on McAdoo's going down to defeat with him. A mutual withdrawal was agreed upon, and the nomination went at last to John W. Davis on the one hundred and third ballot.

Thanks in large part to radio coverage of that seemingly endless convention, Smith's name was now something of a household word; so was the appellation pinned to him by Franklin Roosevelt during the nomination speech—that of "the Happy Warrior." But Al did not come across to the public as happy and lovable at that 1924 convention. His obstinacy in the face of mounting indicators that he could not win the nomination did not enhance his image as a cooperative man and a good loser, and many not otherwise put off by the fact that he was a wet and a Roman began to reexamine their man. Al Smith had a chance to recoup in a closing convention speech, and for a moment it seemed he might, when he cast out a light, clever opening remark that brought laughter to the galleries and relaxation to the delegate rows. But then he launched into a speech that, in biographer Richard O'Connor's words, sounded like a chapter from *The Collected Works of Mayor John F. Hylan**. It was a ponderous, deadly dull recitation of the achievements of the Smith Administration in Albany. Al Smith had made himself the bore as well as the boor.

It was better in 1928, at least through the nomination. The Democrats assembled in Houston, and the Smith forces were so smoothly organized that their leader could stay behind in Albany. The state rollcall had only to go as far as Ohio on the first ballot before it was all over. For the first time in history, a major American political party had nominated a Catholic to be President of the United States. It was an auspicious beginning, but everything quickly turned sour. Smith picked just about the worst person possible as Democratic National Chairman—John J. Raskob. As a Catholic, and papal knight to boot, and as a chief executive of General Motors, Raskob's presence fueled

---

* *The First Hurrah, A Biography of Alfred E. Smith,* by Richard O'Connor, G. P. Putnam's Sons, New York, 1970.

the religious issue for many Americans and pointed up big business's displacement of rural America as the dominant influence in the country. In one choice Smith thus managed to quicken a double phobia.

Then the campaign was a disaster. Smith, overly confident of victory, was slow in launching it, and proceded to make one bad decision after another. For instance, he allowed campaign funds to be poured into inflexibly Republican states like Pennsylvania, an exercise akin to throwing money down abandoned coal shafts. At the same time, the South, that hitherto solid Democratic bastion, was seriously neglected. Decisions such as these cost Al Smith several Southern states, and did not gain him Pennsylvania.

Of course, religion cost, too. The 1928 campaign was the most vicious in American history from a religious point of view. Smith was subjected to burning crosses—the KKK had its revenge—constant insult and a Protestant hysteria that defied credence. There was, to be sure, a distinct Catholic partisanship for Smith. Convent doors were unlocked on election day so that nuns could vote, most of them for the first time in their lives. Also, priests in pulpits were anything but subtle about how Catholics should exercise their franchise. But Catholic partisanship was as nothing compared to Protestant prejudice, noticeably in much of the Protestant press. There it wasn't just Al Smith who was running and the Democratic Party that had nominated him; it was the Pope who was the candidate and the Catholic Church that stood to gain the spoils of victory. The editor of the *Baptist and Commoner,* an Arkansas journal, typified this exotic thinking in an editorial which warned:

> To vote for Al Smith would be granting the Pope the right to dictate to this government what it should do.
>
> A vote for Al Smith would be the sacrificing of our public schools. Rome says to hell with our public schools.
>
> To vote for Al Smith would be to say that all Protestants are now living in adultery because they are not married by a priest.
>
> To vote for Al Smith is to say our offspring are bastards. Are you ready to accept this?

But the extremists didn't have to stew long about a possible Smith presidency. The answer to who would be President came early on the night of November 6, 1928. Americans weren't ready for Al Smith. Hoover garnered 21,392,190 popular votes to Smith's 15,016,443; 444 electoral votes to Smith's 87. It wasn't even close. Badly stung, Smith laid heavy blame for his defeat on religious bigotry. But, in truth, religious bigotry was only one factor in the defeat, and very likely not the absolutely decisive one. "Demon rum," Al Smith's big-city image, his Tammany background, the campaign itself—these were factors also.

Actually, in the final analysis, Smith could have been defeated by Republican prosperity. Americans traditionally vote their pocketbooks, and in 1928 pocketbooks were bulging and the stock market was leaping from peak to peak. Who's going to disturb a good thing? The Republicans, in fact, had so much going for them that H. L. Mencken had to be correct when he wrote: "Hoover could have beaten Thomas Jefferson quite as decisively as he beat Al."

While Al Smith was losing the presidency, Franklin Delano Roosevelt was winning the governorship of New York State, and if the presidential outcome did not seal Smith's fate, Roosevelt's victory did. Smith dallied in Albany for weeks after the Roosevelt accession, not suspecting that the man he had mentored politically would not want to call on him for counsel and advice, particularly with respect to some key aides. No call came. Smith endured the situation as long as he could—which was much longer than was necessary—then went sulking off to his new turf, the country clubs of Florida and his Fifth Avenue apartment. The final straw had come when Roosevelt refused him the courtesy of an advance copy of his first message to the 1929 Albany legislature. Smith had asked to see the message, and Roosevelt had agreed to send it, but somehow it never arrived at Smith's hotel. Al finally woke up to the fact that he wasn't governor anymore.

There was more to wake up to, for it quickly became clear that Roosevelt was not going to be content with Albany and that he had his eyes set on the White House, a vision that had not yet left Al Smith's eyes. In 1931 Smith moved to head off Roosevelt and protect his own chances for another try at the presidency, but the effort was badly organized and, worse yet, disastrously conceived. To stay alive politically, Smith had to contend ideologically with Roosevelt. The difficulty was that Roosevelt had preempted Smith's political and social grounds. Smith, partly thus of necessity but partly, too, by what many saw as a basic conservativism that resided deep in his background, was forced to the right. If it was uncongenial political ground, Smith did not display signs of discomfiture. Eventually he was labeling Roosevelt "demagogic," attacking his programs, and sounding more like Hoover than Hoover himself. He hit bottom with a notorious Jefferson Day speech attacking those (read Franklin Roosevelt) who attempt "to delude the poor people of this country to their ruin by trying to make them believe that they can get employment before the people who would ordinarily employ them are also restored to conditions of normal prosperity." People began to wonder what had happened to Al. The answer was simple. He had waffled on his basic social and political principles. So far as 1932 was concerned, it was no contest. Roosevelt swamped Smith on the fourth nomination ballot: 945 to 190, with 12 votes scattered among also-rans.

Smith stumped for Roosevelt in the 1932 election, but his heart was not in the effort. Roosevelt won, of course, and Smith quietly hoped that he would be summoned to Washington for some key post. After all, the crisis gripping the nation was not very different from the challenges he had faced as governor. Roosevelt never contacted Smith, however, and Smith's feelings hardened. He became active in the right-wing, anti-Roosevelt American Liberty League, and went so far in a 1936 radio address as to accuse the

Roosevelt Administration of being alien and socialistic. The charge was made in the course of a Liberty League dinner at the Mayflower Hotel in Washington. Smith suggested that Roosevelt had established a second Kremlin in the White House, then he moved to his peroration:

> There can be only one Capital—Washington or Moscow.
> There can be only one atmosphere of government—the clear, pure, fresh air of free America, or the foul breath of Communistic Russia.
> There can be only one flag—the Stars and Stripes, or the red flag of the godless union of the Soviet.
> There can be only one national anthem—'The Star Spangled Banner' or 'The Internationale.'
> There can be only one victor. If the Constitution wins, we win. But if the Constitution. . . .
> The Constitution cannot lose! The fact is, it has already won, but the news has not reached certain ears.

Heads shook and voices pitied. Al Smith's support of Alf Landon and Wendell Willkie came as no surprise after that speech. Al Smith's social and political devolution was complete. He had become a side show.

Side shows need a tent, a setting, and Al Smith's was the latest spectacular of the corporate America that had coopted him, the new Empire State Building at Thirty-fourth Street and Fifth Avenue.

The Empire State Building was opened on May 1, 1931, and Al Smith was its chief executive officer and another of its attractions, a complement to the high-speed elevators, observation decks, souvenir shops. Visitors were paraded to his office for a handshake, a cigar, maybe a drink. The more illustrious sat down to lunch and received a personally guided tour of the facility from the man who almost became President of the United States. He was the precursor, in a way, of Philippe Petit, the Frenchman who in 1976 tight-roped between the 110-foot towers of the World Trade Center, further down Manhattan island from the Empire State Building, and of George Willig, the man who scaled the Center's South Tower with mountain-climber's rigging in 1977. But Petit and Willig were one-shot private adventurers, lending a bit of impromptu fame to a business building and making a few bucks out of it in the process. Al Smith didn't have to adventure, at least not in the same way. He was a hired attraction, for $65,000 a year, a colossal sum in those years. All he had to do was spend some time around the place, talk to the boggle-eyed about the Eighth Wonder of the World, and pick up his pay check. Robert Moses, a one-time Smith aide, once rued this occupation. "There were more important things of a public nature to which he might have devoted his energies than running the Empire State Building," Moses was to comment.* No truer words, etc. But Al Smith's bed was of his own making. He had marketed his integrity for money, hired out his

* *A Tribute to Governor Smith,* by Robert Moses, Simon & Schuster, 1962.

presence like the fat man in Barnum & Bailey's Circus, the bearded lady, the guy in the high-wire act.

Jimmy Walker, the playboy mayor of New York and baiter exquisite, once remarked that the Empire State Building seemed like the sort of place "some public official might like to come and hide." Al Smith was not amused, but Walker saw more clearly than did Smith the wherefore of the Empire State Building job.

The travesty continued after Al Smith was dead and gone. (Death occurred October 4, 1944, in the hospital of the Rockefeller Institute.)

In 1945 an Alfred E. Smith Memorial Dinner was inaugurated in New York under the sponsorship of the Cardinal Archbishop, Francis J. Spellman, and with the patronage of a dowager family that picked up the tab so that all proceeds from the $100-a-plate dinner would go to twenty-two hospitals in the metropolitan area, some denominational, some non-denominational. The dinner, held annually in the Waldorf-Astoria Hotel and swish as Southampton, even to real lace tablecloths, was billed as nonpolitical. But year after year politicians parade to it and pundits study guests and speakers, like diviners over tarot cards. When Cardinal Spellman was at the height of his power—when, in other words, Chancery was "the Powerhouse" and the Catholic vote, never a misnomer, was something to contend with—political attention focused on the person tapped by the Cardinal as the dinner speaker. To be invited as speaker constituted a kind of official blessing, more oblique perhaps than an outright editorial endorsement by the *New York Times*, but just as real.

The Al Smith Dinner is less manipulated and manipulative today. The Catholic bloc has fractured and Spellman's successor, Cardinal Terence Cooke, is not the king-maker that Spellman was. Still, in presidential election years, the candidates of both the Democratic and Republican parties play the Al Smith Dinner, mostly for laughs. It's a good showplace, a media event, and maybe with the help of a good speechwriter the candidate can match the wit and sophistication of Jack Kennedy in 1960, when Kennedy lauded Spellman for bringing together two apprehensive political foes. . . . Mr. Richard Nixon and then-governor Nelson Rockefeller of New York. Jack Kennedy noted that *The Wall Street Journal* had criticized Mr. Nixon. "That's like *L'Osservatore Romano* criticizing the Pope," he said.

Kennedy's was a neat, incisive touch, and no one has come close to it since, not even Jimmy Carter, when he confessed to the 1976 gathering that if he ever gave another interview on the Biblical sins of pride and lust—a reference to his controversial *Playboy* interview in which he allowed as he had committed lust in his heart—it would be to a reporter from *Our Sunday Visitor*. Not bad, but not quite Kennedy.

The point is this: the Al Smith Dinner is good for charity, but it only trivializes what's best and good about the memory of the person it is intended to honor. It's a political variation, no more, of the St. Patrick's Day Parade—full of fluff, short of substance.

As such it recalls not one of the greatest Assemblymen that the State of New York has ever known, not one of its greatest governors, not the public administrator of progressive new vision, forfeited though that vision one day was. Instead the Dinner recalls the soft, insubstantial Al Smith—the comic Al Smith who pranced about in a brown derby, wisecracked out of the side of his mouth, puffed cigars incessantly. In a sense, the Al Smith Dinner may be said to be life imitating life. But wipe out those last fifteen years. There was more to Al Smith than he left us. That's the real tragedy of the Al Smith story.

II

WILLIAM HENRY O'CONNELL

The Prince of Yesterday's Prototypes

H IS FATES involved several papacies. His patrons included eminences Merry del Val and Francesco Satolli. In the American hierarchy, his fortunes touched those of Gibbons and Ireland, though his contemporaries, more properly, were Mundelein and Dougherty and Hayes. His foils were lesser breeds of clergy and laity. In his native Archdiocese of Boston, he clubbed with Brahmins when they held all the keys to the city—and he matched wits with Harvard across the Charles, until molified late in life by an honorary degree. He was a great doer and a brilliant administrator; an aesthete; a thunderer. Catholics quaked at his voice, and in Massachusetts the earth shook under his tread. He was physically prepossessing. Large. He was legendary. His shade flits through the *romans à clef* of novelists Henry Morton Robinson and Edwin O'Connor.

This was William Henry O'Connell, rector of the North American College in Rome, 1895-1901; Bishop of Portland, Maine, from 1901-1906; in 1905, special papal envoy to Japan's Emperor Mutsuhito; and from 1906-1944 Archbishop of Boston, thirty-three of those years as cardinal. For three decades plus, the O'Connell remains have rested in a mausoleum on the grounds of St. John's Seminary in Boston's Brighton section; the memory that many expected to be as formidable as the man himself is also at rest—faded, alas, like that of most mortals.

The generations of priests O'Connell raised up are thinned by death and retirement; the seminary that bore his name has been shut for want of applicants; the hymns he composed are no longer sung; and those giant episcopal footsteps—they have been amply filled by prelates of quite different mien. He's much forgotten. I was a boy when O'Connell was an old man and still perhaps the most powerful individual in New England. Yet the only real memory I carry of him is a holiday granted in parochial school for one or another of his anniversaries. William Henry O'Connell has settled deep into the dust of history—and of ecclesiastical prototypes.

It wasn't supposed to end thus. The Boston of his bequeathment was to be another Rome, and though His Eminence would have passed on, there would be his works (living memorials), and those conscientiously preserved sermons, addresses, pastoral letters. Gathered into eleven volumes, these would be the "handbooks of the American clergy and people" for years to come. So Father John Sexton assured us in his biography of O'Connell. So confirmed the *History of the Archdiocese of Boston,** for which O'Connell unabashedly furnished the *imprimatur*. "As all critics

---

* Published in three volumes; by Robert H. Lord, John E. Sexton and Edward T. Harrington, The Pilot Publishing Co., 1945. Cardinal O'Connell provided the *imprimatur* and a foreword before his death.

have recognized," the O'Connell volumes are "outstanding for their vigorous clear-thinking power and beauty of expression, and the superb exposition of Catholic and American ideals," said the *History*. O'Connell did nothing to moderate *this* thinking about *his* thinking. "After all," he wrote as early as 1931 to a young monsignor named Spellman, "it is something to have written and spoken for nearly half a century and never once written or spoken a sentence that was not perfectly orthodox."

As ever, time is the great leveler. The O'Connell books took on the weight of lead. And Boston, of course, never became the new Rome of O'Connell's vision, the curialization of administration and the new buildings on the hilltops, Roman-like, notwithstanding. William Henry O'Connell was a remarkable churchman and a cosmopolitan personality. He spoke several languages, quoted the classics, appreciated the arts, sang snatches of Gilbert and Sullivan, and was as much at home at an organ keyboard as he was at a public library board meeting. Thus, for the George Apleys, he was blessed antidote to that swarm of Irish immigrants who, in the phrase of one social historian, had "slipped into Boston society like a soiled handkerchief into the back pocket." By the same token, he was for Catholic immigrants the symbol of "arrival" and eventual ennoblement. Certainly he provided a height towards which to gaze, whether in admiration, awe, fear, contempt, respect, or combination thereof.

But time can be cruel—or is the word "revealing"?

O'Connell's place in history is obviously not what he envisioned it would be, and in behalf of which he bent certain energies. "There is . . . a certain rightful demand that posterity should not be left merely to guess," he wrote in his preface to *Recollections of Seventy Years,** and therefore he took pains that the record was detailed. It might have been better had posterity been left to presume. Nor is his place in history what certain contemporaries assumed it would be. Obviously it is not that anticipated by biographers: Sexton in *Cardinal O'Connell: A Biographical Sketch*** and Dorothy G. Wayman in *Cardinal O'Connell of Boston****. Critics and historians have taken to print, and though some of their commentary is sometimes as tendentious as the quasi-official views are unreal, one thing is clear: The record is a jumble of distortion; revisionism is in order.

In any second look, O'Connell's genius for administration stands, as always, the closest scrutiny, the hardest assessment. Perhaps, also, his genius in the use of economic muscle. Catholics of Boston, for instance, were much sooner arrived in executive positions, as on the boards of banks, than their counterparts in Worcester or Providence or any other New England city, because O'Connell was disposed, through a few judiciously placed telephone calls, to make the Yankee establishment face up to a fact or

* Houghton Mifflin, Boston, 1934.
** Pilot Publishing Co., Boston, 1926.
*** Farrar, Straus & Young, New York, 1955.

two of the new Boston; namely, that Catholics had not only arrived in the community, but were there to stay. But is O'Connell vulnerable in other respects? This necessitates some unpleasant questions.

For instance, is O'Connell's 1921 pastoral letter on social justice and industrial problems really still "well worth reading," as Mrs. Wayman said it was in 1955? Or is it "balanced" to the point of meaninglessness? And is it in fact badly outdated? The friendliest of rereadings renders Mrs. Wayman's evaluation sanguine, much too buoyant. (It hurts to say that, as Dorothy Wayman, now deceased, was a dear friend.)

Going on, did O'Connell's cultural tastes translate themselves to the populace as a whole? Or were they so rarefied that they actually contributed to the culture gap between Boston's lettered and unlettered? If so, might present-day Bostonians be carrying something of a burden from William Henry O'Connell? Preposterous. Still, it could prove the case if just some theories of William V. Shannon's political and social portrait, *The American Irish* (Macmillan, 1963), are valid.

For example, those cultural attitudes that helped produce the stereotype evoked by the catch-phrase, "Banned in Boston."

No one person brought about Boston's reputation of repression, and the notorious censorship group, the Watch and Ward Society, was of course "Yankee founded." Nevertheless, allow Shannon's rationale and O'Connell becomes accessory to the stereotype for having permitted "the Church's moral teachings to be trivialized and distorted through a politically operated censorship of books, movies, and legitimate plays." O'Connell consistently sanctioned the misuse of public authority in the moral field, Shannon charges, which only served to produce embarrassing anomalies and give the Church and Boston a "bad name" throughout the nation. Thus, notes Shannon, the Old Howard flourished as a notorious burlesque theater in the heart of Boston, while Eugene O'Neill's *Strange Interlude* had to open in a suburban movie house to avoid Boston's theatrical censorship.

Back to social justice. Shannon takes a jaundiced view, accusing O'Connell of giving "no impetus" in the archdiocese to the papal encylcicals, *Rerum Novarum* (1891) and *Quadragesimo Anno* (1931). There was no recognition, writes Shannon, that the overwhelming majority of his fellow Catholics were in the low-income bracket, and that a sizable number of them were unemployed for long periods. "The social problems of Boston called urgently for the Church to leave its ivory tower, and go into the marketplace to spread its social teachings," Shannon argues. "But no such missionary effort was attempted."

Politics. Shannon credits O'Connell with a "dogged assertion of the importance of simple integrity in public office." But even this, Shannon, now an editorial writer and columnist for the *New York Times*, discounts. The effects of O'Connell's efforts were much less than they might have been, he writes, if the emphasis "had been part of a broader message that struck home with real impact in the daily lives of tens of thousands of impoverished, frustrated Boston Catholics in the 1920's and 1930's."

There's a contrary point of view, of course. But its persuasiveness, at one time weakened by obsequiousness, is undercut by an insistence on the part of O'Connell partisans to hold him forever above fault or folly.

Sacco-Vanzetti, the celebrated case involving two Italian immigrants accused of murdering a paymaster for a South Braintree shoe company in 1920. Was Bartolomeo Vanzetti's sister, over from Italy to plead for the lives of the condemned pair, a tool of left-wing and anarchist groups, as was widely charged? More pertinently—whether she was a tool or not—was O'Connell the truly compassionate spiritual leader one would expect him to be when he rejected her tearful plea to intervene with Governor Alvan T. Fuller towards a commutation of the death sentence? The scenario sketched by O'Connellists presents a choice in sympathies between ideological opportunists (the mercy pleaders) and an inflexible prelate who felt he could not "intervene in the process of the law of the land." However one examines the choice, O'Connell comes thorugh as a heavy—the more so since on other issues later in life he had little compunction about influencing the process of law.

The 1924 Child Labor Amendment. Did the proposal in fact usurp "parental rights to child education and control"? Was it indeed "soviet legislation," as O'Connell branded it in a letter to Baltimore's Archbishop Curley? The document is now located in the Catholic University archives. Or was O'Connell's oposition an error in judgment that no amount of explaining can offset? ("Boston is having a brainstorm," one American prelate is reported to have written to another. "He is one against a hundred.")

O'Connell lived in an age when a kind of perfection attached itself to clergy, and to bishops especially. It may have been more handicap than help. In making O'Connell bigger than life, his partisans very probably did him his greatest disservice.

Also, O'Connell's critics may not always have been all so scabrous as sometimes portrayed. It is interesting, for instance, that one of the first of the demythologizers—Jack Alexander, in a celebrated 1941 *Saturday Evening Post* piece, "The Cardinal and Cold Roast Boston"—presents the most defendable rationale for O'Connell's actions on the Child Labor Amendment. "What is generally not known," said Alexander, "is that Cardinal O'Connell would approve the amendment, according to persons close to him, if the word 'gainful' were inserted before the word 'labor' in Section I, which now reads, 'The Congress shall have power to limit, regulate and prohibit the labor of persons under eighteen years of age.'"

The Constitutional amendment never passed, of course, though most of its objectives were eventually gained through extensions of the Fair Labor Standards Act.

As Catholic cleric, William Henry O'Connell traveled a familiar route. He was born in the Massa-

chusetts textile community of Lowell in 1859, the son
of Irish immigrants. The family knew privation,
overcame small tragedies, achieved modest successes,
and gave the brightest of the offspring to God. By the
time "Bill" O'Connell sailed for Rome in 1881 to study
at the North American College, the father was in an
early grave. But there were lace curtains in the parlor
windows, pride in the mother's heart, large ambition
in the son's bosom. Young Bill was to succeed beyond
predictable measure. Intelligence and talent he possessed; fame he attained; riches he came by—including a 1918 bequest worth almost $2.5 million
from the estate of theater magnate Benjamin F. Keith,
whose acquaintance he gained when Keith one day
came inquiring about a papal medal for his Catholic
wife. Great influence would also be O'Connell's: for
two weeks President Harding would delay the appointment of Pierce Butler to the Supreme Court until he
could consult O'Connell.

O'Connell indulged his gifts and his blessings in the
manner of a Venetian doge. He startled Maine by
arriving as bishop in 1901 with "a suite of Italian
retainers": a coachman, Pio Zappa; a music master,
"Count" Pio DeLuca; a valet, Peppino; Peppino's wife
and "curly-headed bambinos." Years later, when a
new archbishop's residence would be built in Boston,
it would be a grand mansion of Renaissance design,
filled with marble chests, carved oak furniture, oriental rugs, large canvases in massive gold-finished
frames, and profuse objects of art—many of which
would be auctioned off by his successor, Richard J.

Cushing, as indeed Cushing would turn the third floor of the "palace" into a dormitory for students whose scholarship he was sponsoring at Harvard and MIT.

In due course, there would be a winter home in Nassau—acquired, by one pious account, "on the advice of physicians"—and a summer home in Marblehead, high on the rocks overlooking the harbor. O'Connell prized his privacy, and from time to time he would have young picnickers ordered off the North Shore rocks. One summer, a wag posted the sign, "The world is the Lord's and the fullness thereof, but the rocks belong to the Cardinal."

The Marblehead home was modest; the Nassau home grand enough to have once belonged to Lord Dunmore, a Colonial governor. The comings and goings thereto inspired the irreverency, "Gangplank Bill."

O'Connell was, in sum, the quintessential prince in a day when princeliness became the episcopacy. Once on entering Boston's Cathedral of the Holy Cross, the berobed, handsome O'Connell caught the words of a female admirer, "He has the face of God!" O'Connell turned to one of his chaplains: "Father, behold the simple faith of our good people." The incident need only be possible to be true.

One winter, before sailing to Nassau, O'Connell put Father Cushing in charge of his pet poodle Moro, with strict instructions about his care. Against all orders, Cushing began feeding Moro scraps from the dinner table: bacon, sausages, eggs, left-over chops, everything. About a week before O'Connell's return, Moro succumbed from his unaccustomed diet. Dilemma: How to tell the old man? Cushing greeted the cardinal and blurted out the bad news, fully expecting to get his head knocked off. "Poor Moro," sighed O'Connell. "He pined away for his absent master."

The issue that brought O'Connell to high place was the "phantom heresy" that masqueraded as "Americanism" but which amounted, in retrospect, to little more than ideological separatism from Rome in the adapting of the Church's teachings to popular manners and modes. Pre-Vatican II-ism, in a sense. O'Connell was not part of the controversy, and conscientiously walked wide of involvement. Thus, where "Americanism" would cost Bishop John J. Keane the rectorship of Catholic University in Washington, and Archbishop John Ireland of St. Paul a red hat, it would be O'Connell's making.

This developed when Roman counteraction to "Americanism" swept Monsignor Denis J. O'Connell—no relation to the Lowell O'Connells—out of the rectorship of the North American College. That O'Connell had become the symbol in Rome of the liberal wing of the American hierarchy; he had to go.

As fortune would have it, William O'Connell's friendly professor of scholastic philosophy from seminary days at the Propaganda—Monsignor Satolli—was now Apostolic Delegate to the United States. Satolli, a favorite of Leo XIII and himself soon to become a cardinal, urged on the Pope the name of the young curate from St. Joseph's parish in Boston's

West End. On November 21, 1895, Leo named the Boston O'Connell to the North American College rectorship. It was an appointment that was not greeted ecstatically. No O'Connell appointment ever was, it seems. The Archdiocese of St. Paul sent six students to the college while Denis O'Connell was rector: it sent not one during William O'Connell's six-year term.

By all Roman measurements, William O'Connell was a huge success as rector. He doubled enrollment (in spite of St. Paul), rehabilitated the college's finances, secured a summer villa for students (at Castlegandolfo, where the Pope, coincidentally, also summered), and won for the college such friendships as that of William Heyward, the bibliophile, who willed his library to the college. More crucially for his career, O'Connell stayed free of "Americanist" taint. He is speared for this by Donna Merwick in her book, *Boston Priests, 1849-1910, A Study of Social and Intellectual Change* (Harvard University Press, 1973). She writes: "Rather than be drawn in as lobbyist for the American church—a role which, as rector of the North American College in Rome, he might have been expected to assume—O'Connell played the royalist, a role that in the eyes of some of the American hierarchy must have seemed the sorcerer's apprentice." Perhaps this was the effect of the O'Connell role, but it should also be said that it was unreal, indeed presumptuous, to have expected him to play any other role than the one he did. O'Connell actually delayed acceptance of the post until after he had visited each of the four archbishops on the college board—Williams of Boston, Corrigan of New York, Ryan of Philadelphia, Gibbons of Baltimore—and obtained assurance that as rector he would not be called upon to serve the interests of any party or group, or do anything that savored of partisanship. For better or for worse, he was consistent in his intent. Unquestionably this suited Rome's purposes fine. But to fault O'Connell for performing as he had virtually pledged to perform, rather than according to the expectations of some, may be investing blame in the wrong place.

When it came time to fill the vacant see of Portland, Maine, in 1901, the choice of O'Connell was as logical in Rome as grace. Again, his was not a popular apointment, as his designation five years later as coadjutor with right of succession in Boston would not be popular. The Maine clergy wanted as bishop one of their own. And when it came time for Boston, the bishops of the New England Province wanted as Metropolitan anyone but O'Connell. Rome, however, liked O'Connell. That was all that mattered.

The road from Portland to Boston was straight and true, although there was almost a detour in 1903 to Manila. The Philippines were now an American possession, a spoil of the war of 1898 with Spain. O'Connell was offered the archbishopric of the primatial see of Manila. He leaned towards acceptance, but was forced to delcine when doubts were raised in some quarters about his patriotism. It was a bum rap. O'Connell had displayed a sympathy for Spain, and had openly stated that the war was unjust—a point on which almost everyone would agree today. But unpatriotic? In the American hierarchial tradition, O'Connell was a superpatriot, and would demonstrate it unmistakably as the years passed. Yet if ever a dark cloud had a silver lining, the Manila episode was it; the loss of that archbishopric was the lucky break of O'Connell's life. The post went at last to Jeremiah J. Harty of St. Louis, who was quickly buried under misunderstanding and strife. Harty resurrected in 1916 as Archbishop of Omaha, but his career was shot. One might presume that O'Connell's would have been too, had Manila befallen him.

To the extent that O'Connell was still under a cloud in 1905, its shadows were whisked away by O'Connell's assignment as a special Papal Legate on a mission to Japan. The assignment provided all the opportunity for redemption that a bishop might have needed in Rome. O'Connell's task was both diplomatic and advisory. He was to ingratiate Rome with the Emperor of this suddenly emerged Oriental power, and he was to survey apostolic possibilities. O'Connell won high marks all around. Japan decorated him with the Grand Cordon of the Sacred Treasure; Pope Pius X ordered all his recommendations adopted, including the founding of a Catholic university at Tokyo to be staffed by Jesuits. Mission accomplished, O'Connell was a shoo-in for advancement. This meant Boston.

O'Connell arrived in Boston in the floodtide of the second great wave of Irish immigrants, and probably his greatest feat as a bishop was in preserving the faith and establishing the presence of the new Irish-American in what was at the time a decidedly hostile environment. Wonderfully quaint and good-natured was the 1905 jingle of Boston as the land of the bean and the cod, where the Cabots speak only to the Lowells, and the Lowells speak only to God. Nevertheless, in the 1900s proper Bostonians still spoke improperly of Irish girls as "kitchen canaries," Irish lads as "Micks," and their children as "shanties" and "muckers." The "No Irish Need Apply" signs were gone, but the blue-nosed *Boston Evening Transcript* was still disposed to accept help-wanted advertisements that specified Protestantism as a condition for employment. The common appraisal—one advance by such a respected church historian as John Tracy Ellis—is that O'Connell was instrumental in reversing the low standing in which Catholics and their Church were held by his own bearing and his performance—as well as by the sense of perspective, spiritual and historical, that he conveyed to the wider Catholic populace. Father Ellis expressed it to me thus, in a letter from Rome, where he was spending the year:

"His superior mind, wise reading and general culture—he knew music well—suggested the cultivated abbé on the grand scale. These talents embodied in a prelate of so formidable size and bearing brought a lifting of spirits, so to speak, in his largely American-Irish flock who felt the need of reassurance *vis-à-vis* their often disdainful Brahmin fellow townsmen. I think it could be said that Boston's Catholics took a certain pride in the cardinal's lofty manner, while they might tremble at the thought of a direct encounter with their archbishop. On his part, the cardinal shrewdly piloted his course in a way to impress both those of Waspish background and his own flock, and that, I believe, is what made him so irate and scornful of (political boss) James Michael Curley, whose dubious goings-on, he felt, were calculated to destroy the very respect O'Connell had set out to win for Boston's and New England's Catholics."

There's minor dissent on the coupling of so-called Catholic "respectability" and O'Connell. Monsignor Francis J. Lally, now of the U. S. Catholic Conference's justice and peace office in Washington but for years editor of *The Pilot*, the archdiocesan newspaper, ticks off the names of O'Connell's predecessors: de Cheverus, Fenwick, Fitzpatrick, Williams. He cites the tolling of the bells of the Protestant churches when de Cheverus returned to France, and Harvard's awarding of an honorary degree to Fitzpatrick in 1861. (In its O'Connell entry, the *New Catholic Encyclopedia* mistakenly identifies O'Connell as the first native Catholic prelate to be so honored.) "O'Connell was coming into a good thing," comments Lally. "I have never been one to believe that O'Connell was the one that made the church 'respectable' in Boston."

The fact remains, however, that O'Connell's immediate predecessor, Archbishop John J. Williams, was so strongly conscious of the "non-acceptability" of Catholics to the dominant Protestant community that he discouraged the building of churches on main streets. It is why, for instance, St. Paul's in Worcester—today the cathedral church of a separate diocese—sits on a side street. A main street site was available, but Williams was anxious not to stir anti-Catholic passions. Even so, construction of St. Paul's created panic for their property values among 1866 Worcester Yankees.

What is indisputable is that O'Connell presided over the Church's full coming of age in Boston, and as the Brahmins withdrew (or were shoved by the sheer pressure of numbers) into the relative obscurity of their banks, their board of directors' rooms and their Cape Ann homes, O'Connell and the church he led moved into the vacuums of leadership and influence.

In administration, the highest marks. O'Connell turned Boston into a model of efficiency during a period of great expansion, and, with the help of the Keith fortune, brought it through the Great Depression with minimum pains. Parishes increased from 194 to 322, and clergy from 600 to more than 1500. Seminary admissions and parochial school enrollments tripled. Three colleges were founded under his sponsorship, and new construction sprouted in all directions. As Boston's immigrant character diversified, O'Connell—a strong Celtophile—welcomed the new arrivals and deplored the "sporadic outbursts of nationalistic feelings" that conveyed a resentment to them—as, for instance, Irish hostility towards Italians, who landed as job competitors, pick and shovel in hand.

O'Connell's influence grew astonishingly, and his power overspilled the ecclesiastical. He could command police escorts. A former *Providence Journal* reporter recalls a motorcycle detail that whizzed the cardinal on a visitation to Fall River. En route from Boston, nature called the cardinal. The chauffer honked for the police to pull over. The police interpreted the honk as a signal to go faster. The chauffer honked again. The police stepped heavier on the gas . . . all the way into Fall River. The cardinal was not amused; he disembarked and, teeth floating, exploded at the startled officers.

O'Connell's temper was notorious. Cardinal Cushing told writer Joseph Dever that he "could turn around and crush with one blow some miserable defenseless little priest, who may have stepped out of line." (Still, "he was the best boss I ever had," Cushing said to Dever. "When he assigned you a job, he let you do it. He would not be looking over your shoulders all the time.") The O'Connell temper could also be withering. A hefty reporter covering one of O'Connell's birthday press conferences—ever a large Boston occasion—had the misfortune of a gilt antique chair's collapsing under him. Snapped O'Connell: "Why didn't you bring an axe?"

In politics, O'Connell kept a low profile, but he was anything but apolitical. Frederick W. Mansfield, a one-time Boston mayor, lobbied about the State House, and on moral issues his voice was widely regarded as that of "Number One," the legislators' cryptology for O'Connell. When preferences stood in danger of being ignored, O'Connell could be blunt. It appeared, for instance, in 1935 that a lottery bill would carry the Massachusetts legislature. O'Connell summoned the press on the eve of the critical vote and condemned the measure as a pure gambling device which "encouraged wagering among the poor, who could least afford it." Overnight, sixty-eight legislators switched their votes. The bill was routed.

On balance, O'Connell preferred indirection, and he was a master at it. When Maurice J. Tobin, an unpaid Boston School Committee member, ran against Curley for mayor in 1937, no one gave Tobin a chance. Curley campaigned breezily in the belief that Tobin was "the softest touch" he had ever had, and on the day before election he bet $25,000 on himself, giving odds of 5 to 4. Election-day morning, however, saw a wondrous page-wide box over the masthead of the *Boston Post*, now defunct but then a staple of the Catholic breakfast table:

VOTERS OF BOSTON:

Cardinal O'Connell, in speaking to the Catholic Alumni Association, said, "The walls are raised against honest men in civic life." You can break down these walls by voting for an honest, clean, competent young man, MAURICE TOBIN, today. He will redeem the city and take it out of the hands of those who have been responsible for graft and corruption. . . .

O'Connell's comment had been made months earlier, but to the quick reader indifferent to quotation marks, the box extended the political blessing of the Cardinal-Archbishop of Boston to Maurice J. Tobin. Curley headquarters was enraged, and an emissary was dispatched to ask O'Connell to disavow this fradulent use of his name. The emissary was kept waiting an hour in an anteroom of the cardinal's residence, then word was sent out by secretary that His Eminence was too busy to see anybody.

The ploy worked perfectly. When one of Curley's ward heelers phoned home at noon to let his mother and three sisters know he was sending a limousine around to take them to the polls, the mother reportedly said, "Don't bother. Coming home from Mass this morning the girls bought a *Post* and there, big as life, His Eminence comes out for young Mr. Tobin. We've already voted for the lad." Curley was defeated by 25,250 votes, the second-worst runner-up showing in Boston history to that time.

Whether O'Connell was party to this business is yet a matter of speculation. He admitted nothing, of course. And *Post* editor Clifton Carberry never let on. "All that is definitely known," Jack Alexander wrote in the *Saturday Evening Post,* "is that on the night before the election there was a telephone connection of some kind between the *Post* city room and the cardinal's residence. The nature of the call has never been revealed."

It is possible to suspect O'Connell's collusion, or at least his acquiescence, for he was not entirely above the shenanigans he deplored in others. Donna Merwick alludes to "falsified experiences" in his *Recollections*; says Dorothy Wayman: "There are a number of factual errors to be found in the pages of *Reminiscences* [sic] *of Seventy Years,*" though she proceeds to put the onus on "proofreaders." In addition, there is the curious tale of *The Letters of His Eminence William Cardinal O'Connell, Archbishop of Boston, Volume I, From College Days, 1896 to Bishop of Portland, 1901*, Riverside Press, 1915. The volume was printed, then withdrawn and all available copies destroyed, apparently after a Boston newspaperman became suspicious about the authenticity of some of the letters. Apparently the letters were "tampered with" in order to indicate prescience on such issues as "Americanism." Today there is no card for the book in the Boston Public Library, though there is a copy in the Library of Congress. There was never a Volume II.

Whatever the full facts of the *Boston Post* affair, there was no love lost between O'Connell and Curley. O'Connell was forever scornful of Curley; Curley, on the other hand, was unconvinced to the very end that O'Connell had not cost him the Ambassadorship to Italy. Ostensibly the Ambassadorship was to be Curley's reward for supporting Franklin D. Roosevelt in 1932. Instead Curley was offered Warsaw, which he refused. The common assumption is that Roosevelt "downgraded" his Curley offer because of O'Connell's disinclination to make known his acceptance of a Curley appointment to Rome.

The O'Connell-Curley relationship has been grist

for the novelist, fascination for the historian, case-study for the sociologist. Small wonder. The parallels were remarkable: sons of immigrants; children of hard times (Curley's father was a hod carrier, O'Connell's a brick mason); each left fatherless as a mere tot; each exceptionally bright and ambitious; each on his own succeeding in the fields most open to first-generation Catholic-Americans—politics and the church. With so much in common, how could there have been such estrangement? Francis X. Curley, the only surviving child of the former mayor, governor and congressman, and late of the Jesuit Order, furnishes theory by way of historical analogy. "I personally in later years have thought of the two as a modern counterpart of Henry VIII (an upstart Tudor) and Wolsey (a butcher's son)." So wrote Francis Curley to me in a letter dated February 13, 1975 (just before he was discovered living on welfare by the *Boston Herald American*). "They had to clash when each reached the top."

By 1911, O'Connell was a cardinal and had gone about as far in the Church as a non-Italian churchman could go. After the death of Cardinal Gibbons in 1921, he was the senior American cardinal, and he held the mythical deanship of the American hierarchy until his death in 1944. By 1944, however, the sun had long since set for O'Connell in Rome. He was born of Leo XIII's time. His high noon came during the reign of Pius X (1903-1914), thanks largely to another friend from Roman days, Cardinal Merry del Val, Pius X's secretary of state. The waning began during the pontificate of Benedict XV, and continued during that of Pius XI, and the sunset was so complete after Pius XII's election that O'Connell was not even in a position to determine his own auxiliary bishop. In 1932 he was sent Francis J. Spellman. O'Connell never cottoned to Spellman, and seven years later, when Spellman was promoted to Archbishop of New York, O'Connell was alleged to have remarked, "This is what happens when you teach the bookkeeper how to write." O'Connell eventually got over his pique. Joseph Dever, for instance, records that as Spellman's ascendancy increased and O'Connell was forced to turn to him as a mediator in matters of vital papal business, he did so "with pragmatic good temper," a talent which Dever credits as a "tribute to O'Connell's objectivity and balance of mind."

O'Connell's career thus had its setbacks and disappointments, but curiously—or not so curiously, really, given then-current ecclesiastical protectiveness—the public was to know little about the greatest one, though it was almost to cost O'Connell the Red Hat he prized as much as life itself. The incident involved a priest-nephew. James P. E. O'Connell was Roman-educated like the uncle; he was ordained by the uncle; and despite what was labeled his "youth and lack of experience," he was raised by the uncle to the chancellorship of the Archdiocese of Boston. It was a clear case of nepotism, but O'Connell might have gotten away with it—he could be brazen—had not the nephew secretly married. O'Connell's adversaries got wind of the situation, and the register was photographed for the private eye of Benedict XV. Decidedly upset, the Pope called O'Connell to account in Rome, confronted him with the evidence about the nephew, chided him on his folly, and told him that the power which gave the Red Hat could also remove it. O'Connell was so dressed down that when he left the Pope's presence he reportedly did not believe he would be allowed to return to Boston. Friends and foes, it is said, watched anxiously in Rome to see what his fate would be. It turned out that O'Connell would go back to Boston, and that the news would be managed so that the American faithful would receive no hint of the scandal.

You won't find this information in the Sexton or Wayman biographies, much less in O'Connell's *Recollections*. Shane Leslie records it in his autobiography, *Long Shadows*, and Leslie is a scholar and observer to be trusted. He adds that "O'Connell, after one terrible scene, cast his nephew away." Mrs. Wayman alludes to this scene in her book, without however providing hints about the nephew's transgression or Benedict XV's threat: ". . .To the sorrow over the defection of any priest," she wrote, was added "the sting of regret for his own blindness in judging character;" making matters worse was a parting scene "embittered with vain remonstrance and angry reproaches."

The humiliation would have bent a frailer man. But

O'Connell was iron. He continued strong and proud to the end, and not without a final triumph or two. For instance, when he entered the Papal Conclave of 1939, it was with the satisfying knowledge that he had made it possible for cardinal-electors to be there from the furthest points of the world. Hitherto, Conclaves were convened ten days after a pope's death, an interval in an era of slower travel that worked against the presence of cardinals from beyond Europe. Twice—in 1914 and 1922—O'Connell missed by mere hours the opportunity to vote in papal elections, and on the second occasion he vented his frustration on the new pope (Pius XI) in an incident famous in Conclave annals. Pius XI ordered the interregnum extended to eighteen days.

On Conclave arrangements O'Connell accordingly left his mark. That mark is less pronounced, however, where it was expected to be the most historic: on the American Church. The 1945 *History of the Archdiocese of Boston* said, "one may safely assume" that when the archives are opened, O'Connell's role will prove to have been a "very important and fruitful one" by reason of his leadership in the foreign mission movement, his long deanship of the American hierarchy, and his presidency of the trustees of Catholic University, to mention just some of O'Connell's involvements. The assumption was sanguine. On some issues O'Connell was enlightened and progressive. He was a youthful admirer of the efforts by Gibbons and Ireland to prevent papal condemnation of the Knights of Labor; he was an early supporter of *Commonweal*, liberal and lay-edited; he was not taken in by Father Charles E. Coughlin, the radio priest—in fact, he saw him, quite accurately, as a "hysterical demogogue." But that same record is spotted by many negative and imperious incidents, such as the demand in 1924 on the chancellor of Catholic University, Archbishop Curley of Baltimore, that he interpose his authority to put an end to the speeches and writings of two eminent priest-professors, John A. Ryan and William J. Kerby. A way was found to do nothing about O'Connell's demand, but the very fact that the attempt at censorship was made reflects seriously on the man. John Tracy Ellis', judgement is harsh, yet inescapable —"The stamp left by Cardinal O'Connell on the church of the nation was faint at best."

Not faint, though, is the stamp left on Boston, and maybe this is as O'Connell himself would have preferred, for he was a passionate believer in the "local church," which he looked upon as the counterpoint to Rome. Cardinal John Wright of the Vatican Curia, a secretary to O'Connell as a young priest, sums up the man in O'Connell's "local-church" concept. "It was the concept of St. Cyprian and of traditional theology generally," Cardinal Wright wrote in answer to a query. "That is, that the polar points in the theological structure of the church are the primate of the Universal Church and the bishop of the local church— and that any structures in between (regional, national or even provincial) are at the most service agencies and by no means should come between the local church (the diocese) and the international church."

This is a concept that has been substantially displaced by Vatican Council II, with its emphasis on national episcopal conferences, lay councils and collegial decision-making—in the ideal realm, if not always the practical. But, of course, O'Connell was a man of his times, not ours. His roots were deeply imbedded in the historical church; his loyalties to decreed tradition were unquestioning. He could not exist today. Yet maybe today owes O'Connell and his type a debt. They are part of what made Vatican II necessary.

III

FRANCIS JOSEPH SPELLMAN

The Powerhouse and the Glory Fading

I LAID EYES ON CARDINAL SPELLMAN only a few times in my life—as in 1964, at the Catholic Press Association convention in New York's Waldorf-Astoria Hotel, when he presented the St. Francis de Sales Award for distinguished service to Catholic journalism to John Cogley; as a year later in the *aula* of St. Peter's Basilica in Rome, just before a general congregation of Vatican Council II. In retrospect, the second sighting was especially symbolic.

Twelve months had taken marked toll. Francis Joseph Spellman, now 76, was quite literally years older than one year before. He appeared from a side door. Short and round, he shuffled across the marble floor towards his seat with the tentativeness of a man in street shoes moving across a frozen pond. He was alone, a lonely figure isolated not by his power but rather its eclipse. Like O'Connell of Boston, Spellman had lived beyond the apogees of influence and authority—by a span of no less than two Popes. Paul VI was reigning; John XXIII was in his grave. Spellman harked back to Pius XII, and in 1965, as much as now, that was a long leap back in history and in glory. So much had happened since Pius XII's death—John's *aggiornamento*, the Council, the debate over Pius's relationships with the dictatorships. Pius

XII belonged to another age. As Pius's "creature"—quite literally—Spellman belonged to another age, too.

Spellman's solitary shuffle was interrupted at last that Fall day in 1965 by a woman journalist with one of those pre-meeting Council passes that gave the uninitiated a feeling of belonging, almost, to the world of initiates. She approached with a greeting, not a question. Question, Spellman probably wouldn't have answered; greeting, he was happy to receive. He responded with the warmth of an aged athlete recognized for some feat of youth.

The irony was that just a decade earlier everything would have been so different. Spellman's close friend would have been on the papal throne, and he, as master of the premier see of the New World, would have commanded attention perhaps next only to that of the Pope himself. Spellman's place was once that large. The retinues that now attended Alfrink of Holland, Suenens of Belgium, Heenan of England would have been his. No longer. This was another day, and Spellman, no fool, knew it. He didn't even believe in the Council—in fact had early predicted to a small group of priests that the Council would produce few changes and that these in no instance would pass the Statue of Liberty. But he was a superb reader of tides, and once it became clear where the currents were going, Spellman moved to adjust. Reform and renewal did not come easily, nor completely, but such as did come were significant. After the first session of the Council, Spellman returned for the crucial debates on religious freedom with the eminent Jesuit specialist on church-state questions as his *peritus,* John Courtney Murray. Like the rest of the world, Spellman knew that for many in Rome Murray represented theological leprosy. Yet here he was at session two with that very person. It must have been delicious for a man with such strong "street smarts" as Spellman. He could satisfy once again the combative impulses that forever resided just below the surface; more particularly, he would have the satisfaction of performing some final, grand service to the Church. Spellman, characteristically, grasped it. Besides, what neater way to upstage the liberals, now obviously in the ascendency, than to whip them at their own game, on his grounds, with their own man?

In any case, no one missed fewer opportunities than this roly-poly man with the high-pitched voice and the deceptively bland Infant-of-Prague manner. Either for Church . . . or for self. "He's the only man in history who catapulted a Brownie camera into a cardinalate," a New York priest recently remarked to me, only half in jest, as we were bundled up against a winter blizzard in the third-floor suite of a Westchester rectory. He was alluding to Spellman's practice, as seminarian at the North American College between 1912 and 1916, of carrying a camera on walks through Rome. Young Frank made it a point of suddenly being in front of the most exalted personalities, asking that they pose for a picture. It was the cleric-as-Big-League-baseball-player-syndrome. "Eventually there wasn't a cardinal in Rome whose picture Spellman did not have in his pocket, ready to be whipped out to be autographed," the priest smiled. Double request, double recognition, maybe double possibility of benefit. After all, cardinals, like the rest of men, are susceptible to ingratiation.

Yet it wasn't a Brownie camera that got Spellman as a young priest back to Rome and moving up the ladder of advancement. It was his pen, and his decision to translate into English two devotional volumes by his old professor at the Propaganda University, Monsignor Francesco Borgongini-Duca. Or could it have been sheer coincidence that, when Spellman was asked back to Rome as director of a playgrounds project funded by the Knights of Columbus, the titular head of the program should have been Borgongini-Duca, then on his way up in the Vatican Secretariat of State? Of course Spellman jumped at the offer, and he became *Addetto alla Segreteria di Stato*, attaché in the first section of the Vatican Secretariat of State.

It was in a Secretariat capacity, and in the company of Cardinal Pizzardo of Curial eminence, that Spellman met the Nuncio to Germany in Berlin in 1929. It was a fateful meeting for Spellman and, as it turned out, for the Church in the United States, as the Nuncio was none other than Eugenio Pacelli, soon to become Vatican Secretary of State and eventually Pope Pius XII. The two struck up a friendship that eventually would carry Spellman to New York and to the pinnacles of ecclesiastical influence. For the time being, however, they would be companions rather than confidants and co-movers in high places. They traveled together and vacationed together—weeks, that is, that were supposed to be vacations but which, in Spellman's words, turned into times "of work and retreat," in places such as Rorschach in the Canton of St. Gallen on Lake Constance and the Institute Stella Maris at Menzingen. The closeness of the relationship was forged during Pacelli's years as Secretary of State, so that when a special situation arose demanding the talents of a special person, the Vatican dialed 'O' for O'Malley . . . errr, 'S' for Spellman.

Once was after Gugliemo Marconi invented the wireless, and loyally presented a fully-equipped transmitting station to the Vatican. The world quite literally hung on the first words that would come from the lips of the Holy Father via this new miracle of communications. At least Catholics of the world did. For them, the occasion was Armstrong on the moon. For Spellman, it was the chance to play Shorty Powers in Mission Control Center; for after Pius XI finished speaking, he was to translate the papal words for the English-speaking world. The moment was auspicious; the words, alas, less then memorable. No "one small step for a man, one giant leap for mankind," comment. Spellman had to cope with such sentiments as, "Hear, O ye heavens, the things I speak. Let the earth give ear to the words of my mouth. Hear these things, all ye nations; give ear, all ye inhabitants of the world, both rich and poor together. Give ear, ye islands, and harken, ye people from afar . . ." Trite. Yet Catholic America was rhapsodic. Bishop Thomas

Mary O'Leary of Springfield, Mass., wrote Spellman: "The transmission was flawless. Your voice was perfect. Your enunciation most distinct, your delivery full of unction and eloquence. What an honor to be selected. . . ."

It was only the beginning of wonders involving Frank Spellman. Six months later came a scenario to challenge Alfred Hitchcock, a comment not made frivolously, for indeed the incident was to make its way into fiction and onto movie screens, the name changed and the drama heightened, but the inspiration being Monsignor Frank Spellman and a mission undertaken at highest Vatican bidding.

It was 1931, the day of the European dictator and of the tyranny of Mussolini and Italian Fascism. The Vatican Concordat was two years old, but already the Vatican felt itself under pressure. Pius XI decided to issue an encyclical which, while definding Vatican concepts of the meaning of Catholic Action, would also condemn racism and the exaggerated nationalism of Fascist political philosophy. The encyclical evolved under the title *Non Abbiamo Bisogno*—"We have no need." Evolving also was concern that the encyclical might fall victim to Fascist censorship. A plan was devised. The encyclical was to be set in type, in great secrecy, in the Vatican printing office, but it would not be issued from the Vatican. The text would be carried out of Italy by trusted messenger for issuance in a country where censorship was out of the question. France was convenient. Who would get it there? Who else but Monsignor Spellman? He would travel by train as a diplomatic courier, carrying a pouch for the Apostolic Delegate of France. With him would be the encyclical, and a note from the Associated Press bureau chief in Rome to his counterpart in Paris. "You may have absolute confidence in the bearer," the note would read. "He is fully authorized to say whatever he says and to do whatever he does. Please offer him every facility of whatever nature he wishes." The rest is history. Spellman contacted not only the Associated Press, but also United Press, International News Service (the two had not yet merged into United Press International), Reuters and other European agencies. *Non Abbiamo Bisogno* sped to the world, its impact quickened by the highly unusual circumstances attending its release, and their reflection upon freedom's condition in Fascist Italy. *Non Abbiamo Bisogno* went out under a Paris dateline, together with the information that the encyclical had been gotten there by a junior official of the Vatican Secretariat of State. Our Man. Spellman was very much hero and international celebrity. There was some nervousness that he would not be allowed back into Italy, but he returned to Rome without incident, his future more assured than ever.

It is no secret what Spellman wanted his future to be. Letters home, unblushingly made available to Father Robert Gannon for his authorized biography (*The Cardinal Spellman Story*, Doubleday, 1962), saw the future in terms of the episcopacy. Spellman was as anxious for a miter as a young kid for a baseball glove.

When the Manchester, N.H., diocese opened up, Spellman had an eye on it. Portland, Me., as well. Instead, to Cardinal O'Connell's great dismay and what was probably his own qualified satisfaction, Spellman was named Auxiliary Bishop of Boston. The date was July 30, 1932. He chose to remain in Rome for his consecration the following September, whereupon he sailed back to the insulting greeting—WELCOME TO BOSTON. CONFIRMATIONS BEGIN ON MONDAY. YOU ARE EXPECTED TO BE READY. CARDINAL O'CONNELL—and the uncertainties of an episcopacy under a boss who regarded him with less than affection. Indeed, O'Connell considered Spellman hardly more than a ribbon clerk, and made the point clear time and again.

Engraved in Spellman's mind were earlier humiliations: the assignment, as a young priest back from five years' study in Rome and possessed of a doctorate in sacred theology, to the staff of *The Pilot*, the archdiocesan newspaper, not to write editorials and edit news, but to pump up subscriptions by preaching in a different church Sunday after Sunday; the assignment at last to Chancery, but only as an archivist working in a basement office. Lest the signals be unclear, there was that letter, received during this period, from Monsignor J. P. E. O'Connell, the Cardinal's nephew and the archdiocesan chancellor: "I trust it will not be wasted advice to suggest to you that it may be well, while you are yet in the beginning of your career, not to allow yourself to get any false conception of your importance, or the importance of your particular work, thus leading you to either the one extremity, temerity, or the other, timorousness. I make this statement because one of your recent letters to me savored of arrogance, a quality which ill befits a subordinate. I passed it over without comment at the time because I attributed the display to your callow inexperience. A change in the attitude which you have so far displayed to my personal knowledge will have wholesome effects for yourself in the future."

The letter was signed by the nephew but it represented the mind of the uncle, if not his actual authorship. In any case things would be little different when Spellman was Auxiliary Bishop. He became, almost in literal fact, the Confirmation machine O'Connell gave threat of his becoming in his shore-to-ship telegram: over the next seven years he would confirm, by count, 177,141 Catholics young and old, no doubt something of a record. He would also be assigned to live in the seminary, a detail, in Gannon's words, "that underlined the Ordinary's coolness." For five months Spellman held his peace, then when Sacred Heart parish in Roslindale opened up, Spellman put in his request for it. O'Connell let the request sit for over two weeks, then sent a letter by hand, with instructions that the bearer await answer, naming him pastor of Sacred Heart parish—but in Newton Center, not Roslindale. The fortunes of the two parishes have shifted in the years since, but in 1933 Roslindale was a far more desirable appointment than Newton Center. Spellman was furious. Yes, he would accept the Newton Center assignment, Spellman wrote back, "but frankness and fairness oblige me to state that I would prefer to remain where I am, if I have the alternative. I would be pleased to go to Roslindale but if Your Eminence has determined otherwise, I shall endure the humiliation of seeing some priest appointed to a better parish than the Auxiliary Bishop." It was a tough letter, and one which some cite as an example of the peevishness which demeaned so much of what could have been ennobling about Spellman. Years later, a Spellman clerical aide brought the letter up with him, gently suggesting that the letter might have been intemperate. "Well," said Spellman, "he deserved it, the way he treated me." In point of fact, O'Connell did deserve it.

It is also true, however, that if anyone had written a letter like that to Spellman after he became Archbishop of New York, he would have ended up missing vital parts.* Indeed the provocation sometimes need not have been anywhere near so direct for Spellman to have visited his displeasure on a person. Father John K.

---

* Spellman was appointed to New York on April 15, 1939. It was one of the first acts of the new Pope, Spellman's old friend—Pius XII, né Eugenio Pacelli. According to insiders, the name of Archbishop John T. McNicholas of Cincinnati had been submitted to Pope Pius XI to fill the see left vacant by the death of Cardinal Patrick Hayes, but the nomination was still on his desk, unacted upon, when Pius XI himself died. Pius XII left McNicholas in Cincinnati and tapped Spellman in Boston for New York. Because no consistories were held during World War II, it was not until February 18, 1946 that Spellman was raised to the cardinalate.

Daly was removed as Catholic chaplain at Columbia University in 1956 and dispatched to the boondocks simply for writing a literate and generally favorable critique in *Commonweal* of Lionel Trilling's *Freud and the Crisis of Our Culture*. And Father Daniel Berrigan, S. J., was dispatched to Latin America for co-founding in 1965 the peace group that began as Clergy Concerned About Vietnam, Spellman intervening with Berrigan's superiors to bring about the "exile." In the first instance, it was rigorous adherence to Roman orthodoxy—Freud and psychiatry being dirty words in the 1956 Church—that impelled Spellman's action against Daly; in the second, it was his special, knee-jerk patriotic instincts. Since 1939 Spellman had been Military Vicar of the Armed Forces of the United States, a post that took him each Christmas season on highly publicized visits to the troops at some extremity of the world, trips which he obviously relished, their exhausting nature notwithstanding. No, Dan Berrigan wasn't going to raise questions about an American war in his archdiocese.

It is said that Spellman valued the office of Military Ordinary more than that of Archbishop of New York, a claim that would probably never have stood the test of a choice between the two posts. Nevertheless, the fact that the notion could even be proposed clues to something basic about the man. He was a rabid anti-Communist and a dyed-in-the-ermine patriot. It is up to the psychohistorian to determine how much of this was due to Catholicism *per se*, and how much to environmental influences, such as those of his native Massachusetts, where the aspersions of WASPs on the loyalties of those of Irish-Catholic background helped make so many into hyper-patriotic Americans. In any case, in the 1940s and the 1950s, when the nation was respectively in fervor and fever over war and ideology, Spellman's anti-Communism and patriotism served him well. Ironically these were to trap him in the 1960s into the foolishness of the Berrigan action and the embarrassments of the Vietnam era, early in the trumpeting of the Catholic leadership there, later in the quoting of Stephen Decatur's toast, "Our country, right or wrong," while on a visit to that unhappy land. Inevitably the critics had a field day. Artist-caricaturist Edward Sorel, for instance, sketched Spellman for The Bestiary series that appeared in *Ramparts* magazine in 1965-66. His subject appeared as a bird, a cardinal naturally, *Spellmanus Bellicosus*, winging past St. Patrick's Cathedral towards the open sea, olive branch in mouth, rocket in claws, and trailing the Spellman quotation, "In religion alone lies the hope for lasting peace." In the specification, *Spellmanus Bellicosus* was said to make "periodic migrations to the feeding stations along the Potomac where he is always welcomed by the local Hawks who enjoy hearing him sing the praises of Franco-birds, McCarthy-birds and Diem-birds."

The satirization is savage, and deserved. But, in fairness, Spellman was not slavish to his impulses, nor was he policeman in the archdiocese for regimented order and decorum. Things happened in New York that cut against the grain of his composition, many because he let them happen. Father George Barry Ford was cassock-deep in ecumenical and brotherhood causes in darkest pre-Vatican II days; Ivan Illich never had the troubles in New York that he subsequently had in Puerto Rico and Mexico; Dorothy Day and the people of the Catholic Worker movement functioned without Chancery hindrance; and when Spellman died in 1967, *Commonweal* had to concede, "he let us alone." At a time when independent lay Catholic journalism was even more of a rarity than it is now, non-interference was no small blessing to count.

Beleaguered priests—at least those not beleaguered by himself—found a friend in Spellman, and he would go the long mile with them, although this sometimes meant encountering serious opposition from powerfully placed conservative churchmen. Thus, in the early 1960s, he stood firm for a New York priest, Myles M. Bourke, who was teaching the New Testament at Dunwoodie, the archdiocesan seminary, and who had written for the April, 1960, *Catholic Biblical Quarterly* an article on the infancy narrative of St. Matthew's Gospel. The article was not primarily about the historicity of the narrative, but that question was dealt with and Bourke's remarks were regarded by some Church "CIA-ers" as "dangerous." The article was delated to the Holy Office, and Cardinal Ottaviani, the Lord High Executioner there, suggested to Spellman that Bourke be removed from the seminary faculty. Spellman refused.

"At that time very little had been written on the infancy narratives by Catholic scholars," Bourke said in a recent letter, "and the Roman reaction was, I suppose, to be expected. As it turned out, the famous first draft of Vatican II's Constitution on Divine Revelation contained a condemnation of such 'errors' as I and a few others had proposed. I know that Cardinal Spellman was prepared to speak in the Council against the condemnation, but I do not know whether the papal decision to have the draft returned to committee came before his intended intervention. As you know, the newly submitted draft was quite different from the first, and had nothing about condemnation of the 'errors.' "

While this was transpiring, Spellman submitted Bourke's name to the Vatican for appointment as a papal chamberlain with the title Very Reverend Monsignor. Spellman subsequently told Bourke "that the nomination was opposed by the Apostolic Delegate Egidio Vagnozzi, the Secretariat of State and the Congregation of Seminaries, and that he never had such difficulty in getting that rather modest honor conferred on any other priest." But he persisted and the appointment was made. Beyond any personal kindness, Spellman's action was important, in Bourke's opinion, because it gave "much needed support to the biblical movement in the Catholic Church at a crucial time."

Other priests have similar stories to tell. In the

mid-West was a New York priest who had succumbed, as they used to say, to "hankering for the Seventh Sacrament." Spellman located him, traveled hundreds of miles to talk to him, only to have the door closed in his face. Subsequently the priest came to New York and apologized for his rudeness. He was reconciled and Spellman secured a place for him in a New England diocese.

Better known is the story of Bishop Bonaventure F. Broderick, a priest of the Diocese of Hartford, Conn., who fell afoul of ecclesiastical authorities while serving as an Auxiliary Bishop of Havana, and who ended up keeping a gas station in Millbrook, N.Y., about eighty miles from New York City. Gannon's biography lays out the correspondence detailing the reconciliation of Broderick after thirty years in ecclesiastical limbo, and his rehabilitation as a bishop, and it is impossible to read that segment of Gannon's book (*The Cardinal Spellman Story,* pp. 146-151) without admiration for the man who was both reconciler and rehabilitator. Rescued from his gas pumps, Broderick was first given a hospital chaplaincy by Spellman, then, in the years before his death in 1943, a wider role as an Auxiliary Bishop and vicar for religious.

Spellman's was a compassionate action correcting an injustice that had resulted largely from misunderstanding. After reassignment to the United States from Cuba, Broderick found himself without see or job, and had written to the Vatican saying that his situation would appear in American Catholicism as something of a scandal. Broderick wished to stress the lack of assignment, but the Vatican—more particularly, Pope Pius X, then reigning—interpreted the comment as a threat to cause scandal, and accordingly put him adrift to suffer until Spellman came along.

There were others who were helped. It is well known, for instance, that in his role as Military Ordinary, Spellman would go to the very top to correct an injustice when he thought a Catholic chaplain had been treated unfairly.

To further give Spellman his due, he was an astute administrator. Of course he was fortunate enough to have on the Chancery staff a priest with a Wall Street background, Monsignor J. Francis McIntyre, later the notoriously conservative Cardinal-Archbishop of Los Angeles. As the man says, it's always nice to have a genius around the office. Still, Spellman possessed a real business acumen of his own, and he was to bring the Archdiocese of New York out of the $28 million debt in which he found it in 1939, to a point by 1967 where it would be sound enough to weather the economic storms of the 1970s in relatively good shape, unlike so many other large sees in the United States.*

---

* Under Spellman, as with all churchmen in those days, church finances were deeply guarded secrets. The laity were to give, not to know. In 1972, however, the Archdiocese of New York, under Spellman's successor, Cardinal Terence Cooke, made public a comprehensive financial report, the first of its kind in the Catholic Church in the United States. The report set net worth of the Archdiocese at $643 million, counting plant and current and endowment fund balances.

Within four months of his arrival, Spellman had the archdiocese on its way to solvency. He amalgamated liabilities, renegotiated interest terms with banks, then made Chancery a low-interest bank of its own for archdiocesan parishes and institutions. Almost overnight, he had lopped $500,000 off annual expenses. To come were a central purchasing agency, a consolidated insurance service, a building commission, and other efficiencies. There would also be innovative fundraising events such as the Cardinal's Christmas Party and the Alfred E. Smith Memorial Dinner, for projects such as the New York Foundling Hospital and St. Vincent's Hospital, downtown.

Meanwhile, the bite was being put on wealthy New Yorkers, privately if not always subtly. Spellman's tactics were considerably different from those, say, of Archbishop Richard Cushing of Boston. Cushing could stand before crowds and get them to peel their socks off for him. Spellman, never a spellbinder and physically unprepossessing in any assemblage, preferred small groups and a flanking operation aimed at the inside breast pocket. A one-time aide recalls a luncheon arranged for five of the city's wealthiest Jewish leaders: "Spelly wasn't eating his lunch and B ____ remonstrated with him and asked what was the matter, and Spelly said in his simpering way, 'I spent $250,000 yesterday for a piece of property in Harlem where the kids could play and keep off the streets.' And he said he didn't have the money for it. B __ said, 'Your Eminence, do you mean to tell me that a man of your stature in this city is going to lose his appetite over $250,000, when you have five men around this table who can take care of that right now?' Then, picking up the gauntlet, B— said, 'R —, are you good for $50,000?' and R— said, 'You bet I am.' B— went down through the three others, and in the space of five minutes Spelly had five checks for $50,000 apiece, and with that his appetite came back and he polished off that lunch like he was a truck driver." This unfailing ability to raise money from Jewish New Yorkers would one day prompt a key organizer for the United Jewish Appeal to remark with envy, "Oh, Spellman was the greatest *shnorrer* (beggar) of us all."

Yet there was nothing in any of this that was personally avaricious. Spellman had about him relatively little of the triumphalism of an O'Connell of Boston or of a Mundelein of Chicago, and his life style was never such as to embarrass priests or laity. Even the aide who shared the luncheon story speaks of the simplicity of his life. "The food at his table was awful and it never seemed to bother him," he remarked. He added in the same breath that Spellman could be "generous to a core, as every chaplain and missionary will attest." Said the priest, "I would be surprised if his personal estate were anything above what an ordinary priest would have attained in the same number of years as Spelly in the priesthood."

Indeed, he was basically so good and talented that those close to him regret the more that he did not take advantage of the first-rate men that he had in such impressive number in the Archdiocese. They might have saved him from the intellectual blunders that eventually diminished him so substantially, or at least have blunted the effects of those blunders. But Spellman was on another wave length. "He seemed always to be uneasy in the presence of strong intellectual people," one priest commented. "That perhaps showed a reflection of his own lack of scholarship, and it hurt him in the end. In a certain sense he was always on the make and those people in the long run are caught up in their own nets. He was a man of simple Faith and I think he convinced himself over the long run that his simplicity had the quality of greatness, without his ever being disturbed by the prospect that others found it a negative thing."

A harsh judgment, but not a totally invalid one. Father John Tracy Ellis, the widely respected Church historian and one who has spent most of his mature life in the academic world, made something of the same point to me. "It would be pleasant to record that Cardinal Spellman was a consistent upholder of all that pertained to academe." That, however, would be "quite unreal," Ellis declared in a letter.

By way of example, before a gathering of sports writers Spellman could regale his audience by making light of honorary degrees from universities, at the same time exalting the sports award he was making to one of their number. Then, with no embarrassment whatsoever over his inconsistency, he could turn around and solicit from a Catholic institution in the Archdiocese an honorary degree for someone he was personally anxious to see honored, such as Cardinal Thomas Tien, Archbishop of Peking.

"He was a popularist," one priest remarked, "and his books prove the point. He didn't know what true intellectuality was." A Spellman speech-writer substantiates the point. "He could murder—I mean really murder—a sentence, a paragraph, a speech," this person recalls, not only by his delivery, which everyone agrees was bad, but by "Spellmanizing" the text, insisting, for instance, on appending one of his "poems." The effect, this priest comments, was like that of seeing "a Titian cut up into long ribbons."

"He had no literary sense at all," this priest continued. "One day at lunch, before rather distinguished people, he announced that he was going to compile an anthology of favorite poems. . . . To give you a measure of his literary range, he announced on that occasion that his favorite lines were:

> Lives of great men all remind us
> We can make our lives sublime,
> And, departing, leave behind us
> Footprints on the sands of time."
>
> *A Psalm of Life*
> Longfellow

For all of that, it was, on balance, a good period for the Church. It was, in fact, the American Catholic Church's era of "the imperial presidency"—New York being Washington, and Spellman being symbol and spokesman for all the people, all Catholics, our "Roosevelt" as it were. King-maker, he certainly was. As Gannon was to say in his biography, never would Frank Spellman have dreamed in 1939 that over the next twenty years so many of his brother-priests would be consecrated before the high altar of St. Patrick's Cathedral. The number was not only large, but in many cases legendary, for better or for worse. There was O'Boyle of Washington, Griffiths of the Military Ordinariate and the United Nations, McEntegart of Catholic University and subsequently Brooklyn; further away, McIntyre, of course, of Los Angeles, Brown of Bolivia, Kennally of the Caroline and Marshall Islands. The roll goes on and on. "Several of his choices were open to question," Father Ellis declared to me, "but in the overall, one cannot, I think, say he abused his power and brought into the episcopacy favorites with little qualification for the rank." It is a gracious and sanguine appraisal, and characteristically John Tracy Ellis, but one that people might wish to challenge in places such as Washington and Los Angeles.

The key, of course, to Spellman's vast ecclesiastical influence was Pius XII, who reigned from 1939-1958. Their long friendship made Spellman someone to conjure with, and even Franklin Delano Roosevelt, the "Spellman" in Washington, did not miss the "signs of the times." He cultivated Spellman, and used his services, although it is not always clear how substantively. In 1943, Spellman went on a six-month, 46,000-

mile tour of Africa and Europe, as Military Ordinary and with travel orders reading "Personal Representative of the President of the United States." World War II was on, and the press speculated that Spellman was a "possible go-between for peace negotiations between Italy and the Allies." Indeed, part of the media saw Spellman's "hand" in the downfall of Mussolini. On Spellman's return, a reporter sought to pin him down. "There have been persistent rumors . . ." he began. "There have been some persistent reporters," Spellman interjected, heading off question and questioner.

To Roosevelt, Spellman was "my favorite bishop"* and unquestionably he was Roosevelt's quiet intermediary in some affairs involving the Vatican. The two

---

* Francis Spellman and Franklin Roosevelt shared a passion for stamp collecting, and in James A. Farley, Roosevelt had a Postmaster General and Spellman a loyal diocesan anxious to feed their habits. Farley hyped-up the collections of both with low-circulation commemorative stamps that acquired instant value by their limitation. Spellman was a stamp-buff from seminary days in Rome, and over the years assembled a priceless collection, particularly in the area of religious stamps: cathedrals, Madonnas, saints, including a Nicaraguan special issue featuring none other than himself. In 1954 Spellman imparted his collection to Regis College in Weston, Massachusetts, in tribute to an aunt who was a member of the Sisters of St. Joseph for more than fifty years. The order runs the college. Regis has spent the years since trying to keep thieves away. The Spellman collection, housed in a museum building on the campus grounds, has been hit a couple of times, most spectacularly in 1959 when, with Brinks-like precision, stampnappers made off with a select lot valued then at some $100,000.

were friends to the end, although Spellman had increasing misgivings over American war policies in Italy—like the Vatican, Spellman would have preferred that the war be waged a safe distance from every shrine on the peninsula, as if this were possible—and further misgivings over Roosevelt's deference to Stalin. Spellman was opposed to any concessions to Communism, and it bothered him that Roosevelt should have gone more than halfway to meet Stalin at Teheran. When Yalta happened, Spellman was virtually floored. "The Archbishop in his office on Madison Avenue knew no more than the general public of what was going on behind closed doors somewhere in the Black Sea area," Gannon was to write, "but when he found that his President had traveled 5700 miles, not to a neutral spot but to Russia because the Red dictator refused to leave home, he felt the humiliation as most Americans did." Roosevelt was to die a few weeks after his return, and as details of the Yalta agreements became known, misgiving was to grow to phobia for Spellman, as for so many other Americans: the Russians are coming, the Russians are coming.

"Providentially," a saviour would walk onto the stage of history who ostensibly would save the nation and God's people from atheistic Communism. He came in the form of a Senator from Wisconsin, with the name Joseph R. McCarthy.

There was more caution in Spellman's public attitude towards McCarthy than there was in that of some other American bishops, but there was no doubt about Spellman's basic feeling of friendship and ideological kinship for the Senator. Spellman may have striven for discretion, but the tilt was pronounced and this became statement in itself. "I have never met Senator McCarthy," Spellman was to say at a press conference in Milwaukee in 1953. "I have never had any telephone conversations with him or received a letter from him. I have never seen him on television. All I know is what I read in newspapers. There are three things I will say about Senator McCarthy. He was a Marine, and having been with the Marines myself, the fact that a man was a Marine places him very high in my book as regards patriotism. He is against Communism and he has done and is doing something about it. He is making America aware of the danger of Communism. He has been elected Senator from his native State, and no one is known better than by his neighbors. I am willing to accept the verdict of the citizens of Wisconsin concerning Senator McCarthy." This was all the cue American Catholics—and many others, for that matter—needed that McCarthy was *bona fide*, that his was a religious and politically authentic response to the challenges of the Cold War, that he was a person to be supported.

Spellman was never to repudiate McCarthy, so it is perhaps no small coincidence that a Mass in McCarthy's honor should have become a St. Patrick's fixture in the years after McCarthy's death. In 1977, three hundred and fifty friends and supporters were still gathering at the cathedral for the Mass commemorating the anniversary of the death of the demagogue from Appleton, Wisconsin. It was the twentieth annual observance.

These years after World War II were not particularly kind to Cardinal Spellman. There was controversy after controversy, each more avoidable than the one before. He clashed with labor in 1949 over a cemetery strike, emptied the seminary classes at Dunwoodie, and personally led the students through the picket lines to dig graves. He clashed with the film industry over art and decency, and climbed into the pulpit of St. Patrick's Cathedral to denounce the relatively innocent movie *Baby Doll*; he had not been in that pulpit since he had condemned the jailing of Hungary's Cardinal Mindszenty several years before. But the biggest flap of all, and the one that proved most personally devastating to his reputation, came with his run-in with Eleanor Roosevelt in 1949 over aid to education.

The issue was basic. Spellman was convinced that Catholic schools would be forced out of existence unless they received government assistance, to which he held they had a right; Mrs. Roosevelt held that the separation clause rendered aid to church-related schools unconstitutional. At the time Mrs. Roosevelt was writing a widely-syndicated column, "My Day," and therein speaking her mind. Spellman, bristling at her views, unleashed a public letter. It was long, emotional, dramatic, and it ended thus: ". . . I shall not again publicly acknowledge you. For, whatever you may say in the future, your record of anti-Catholicism stands for all to see—a record which you yourself wrote on the pages of history which cannot be recalled—documents of discrimination unworthy of an American mother." Naturally, Mrs. Roosevelt denied the anti-Catholic charge; she pledged that she would "continue to stand for the things in our government which I think are right"; then, with aplomb, she stated. "I assure you I have no sense of being 'an unworthy American mother.' The final judgment, my dear Cardinal Spellman, of the unworthiness of all human beings is in the hands of God." The exchange was the news sensation of the day. And why not? How often is a First Lady, former or not, branded "unworthy" by a First Prelate?

"He was doomed from the start on that one," a former Spellman aide, who insisted on anonymity, said to me, "and no amount of persuasion would steer him off—and I know of some prominent people, Bernard Baruch for instance, who tried to no avail. He lost that one hands down and in the end had to go to Canossa to his own humiliation and to the high glee of Eleanor. He didn't think he lost that battle but he surely did, and he lost an immense amount of prestige in New York City among people he thought were his friends."

If anything, the last is understatement. The loss in prestige was grave, and extended beyond New York to the country at large. People for the first time began to wonder seriously whether they had a fanatic on their hands, and their unease was not lessened by Spellman's continuing forays onto battlegrounds. He was as at home fighting secular interests as he was new currents in the Church. Doubts grew stronger, but Spellman's power showed no signs of waning soon. Nor did it. Pius XII would be around until 1958, and he was almost a blank check to security and influence.

Indeed, it would be several years after the deaths of the two of them, and almost to the mid-1960s, before even non-Catholic New Yorkers would feel comfortable about bypassing the "Powerhouse," as Spellman's Chancery was known.*

Inevitably Spellman ended up isolating himself. The world was changing, and political leaders came to the realization that churchmen like Spellman were more to be humored than heeded. Similarly, the new generation of priests and laity found not only that an unbridgeable gap had opened up between them and leaders like Spellman on almost everything from lay initiation to liturgical practice to ecumenical relations;

---

* Monsignor George A. Kelly dates the demise of Catholic political power in New York from the election of Mayor John V. Lindsay in 1965. Shortly after, he writes, "political appointments to municipal agencies servicing poverty, education, health or social welfare were made with scarcely any reference at all to the presence in New York of 3,000,000 Catholics." [The Parish, as seen from the Church of St. John the Evangelist, New York City, *1840-1973*, St. John's University Press, 1973]

wonder of wonders, they also awoke one morning to a Church with a Pope who was more receptive to their notions than those of churchmen like Spellman. For all practical purposes, Spellman was dead the day John was elected, October 28, 1958. It was only the formal, final obsequies that remained to be held.

Still, the last nine years were not unfruitful ones. At Vatican Council II, Spellman was the *de facto* spokesman of the American Church, a detail demonstrated by his one hundred and thirty-one interventions, about a third of all those made by American prelates. However, Spellman's voice was not a prominent one, or at least not a compelling one. This should not have been surprising. "He was as free of ideas as a frog is of feathers," Father E. Harold Smith, a priest of the Archdiocese, was to say in another context. How could it have been different at the Council? In point of fact, no single intervention of Spellman equalled in importance his decision to bring John Courtney Murray to the second session. But give him credit for that.

In these final years, John XXIII was the epitome of kindness, to Spellman as to all others. So was Paul VI, who also provided Spellman with his last hurrah. This came when Paul flew to the United States in 1965 to speak before the United Nations. Not since the visit of the Vatican Secretary of State in 1936—Cardinal Pacelli, later Pius XII—had Spellman been in such a happy position. Then he was escort, companion, guide. Now he was host and squire to a Pope, and he did not overlook a single opportunity, including a liturgical spectacular in Yankee Stadium, to impress visitor, country, world. If ever there was a triumphal hour of hours in Spellman's life, this was it. However, it was symbolic of all that had happened in church and world since Francis Joseph Spellman had been ordained a priest in 1916 that the importance of Paul VI's visit, for the moment and for history, was invested in what took place at the United Nations, not at Yankee Stadium, St. Patrick's Cathedral or any other stops arranged by archdiocesan authorities.

Francis Joseph Spellman was undoubtedly aware of that fact, and as surely as any development that came out of the Council, it must have convinced him that the future was here, that he belonged to the past. In any case, after the Council he offered to resign as Archbishop of New York. Pope Paul asked him to stay on. He did. The stay lasted two years. He died December 2, 1967.

IV

LEONARD FEENEY

The Dragon Turned Reluctant

THE DISTANCE FROM HARVARD SQUARE to Harvard Town is a smooth thirty miles. But for Leonard Feeney and some seventy Slaves of the Immaculate Heart of Mary—the religious order into which the former Jesuit's followers grouped themselves—it was a distance of quarter-century and a rough passage to a better world. Or so it was by 1972. Behind was the nightmare of a theological and disciplinary contention that began in the 1940s in Harvard Square, and climaxed tragically in Rome a decade later. As compared to the past, the present was Eden-like. In a corner of the Town of Harvard called Still River, and in a section of Massachusettes that the superhighways somehow had not found, the Feeney people lived quietly and serenely, still convinced of what they call "the doctrine"—the theory that outside the Catholic church there is no salvation—*extra ecclesiam nulla salus*—and as self-assured as ever in the validity of the doctrinal positions that once made them notorious and brought down on their heads the castigations of ecclesiastical authorities, from Boston through to the Rome of Pope Pius XII.

By 1972, there were no more epithets flying around; no more battles with religious superiors; no more worries about censure, interdiction or other ecclesiastical penalty; no more badgerings from emissaries of various stations to obey, repent, recant, shut up. Leonard Feeney had been put beyond Rome's reach by Rome's ultimate thunderbolt, an excommunication which by then was twenty years old. If this had its personally distressing aspects for Leonard Feeney—as assuredly it did—there was the counterbalancing consolation of resolution. There was also the satisfying suspicion that the weight-on-mind for the excommunication pronounced rested heavier on Rome than on himself and his followers.

In Still River, the Feeney community lives on in Tridentine orthodoxy and righteous satisfaction. The peace that is theirs is vindication of their orthodoxy, just as the ferment in the wider church is confirmation in the real order of all they warned against if the church continued on a laxist course away from *extra ecclesiam nulla salus*. It is all the evidence the community needs that theirs was the right doctrinal course; for them the onus is on "salvation-liberals" and on those who dealt with them so harshly. In their hearts they know they were, and still are, right.

The Feeney people do not argue their doctrine any more. They have long since wearied of that. They still take to the road to sell the dollar books once so important to their economy (more so than now), but more and more their world is a cluster of white frame buildings (the main house dates from the French and Indian War period) strung along a rural Massachusetts road that few other than townsfolk travel these days. There the Feeney people live amidst a mountain of Latin and Greek books, first-class relics (685 of them, a virtual graveyard), antique wood carvings (quite fine), and a welter of religious art such as to boggle the eyes of an indiscriminate pre-Vatican II collector.

This is the latter-day St. Benedict Center, successor to the converted furniture store at Bow and Arrow Streets in Cambridge, hard by Adams House and Harvard Yard, which served as the original St. Benedict's, seedbed of the chapter of American Catholic history known as the Boston Heresy Case.

At the first St. Benedict's, the Feeney people exercised an aggressive evangelism. They also engaged in a busy defensive operation: watchdogging Boston Catholicism, hounding archdiocesan and Jesuit officials, excoriating Harvard University, anathematizing Protestants, damning Jews—until Rome at last considered itself goaded into proclaiming Feeney excommunicated, something it obviously preferred to avoid.

At the second St. Benedict's, the Feeney people live and let live. Their focus is largely themselves: their purpose, their individual salvations. Theirs is a life of withdrawal according to a rule which is strongly Benedictine in character, but also evocative of the transcendentalism that washed across New England intellectualism in the nineteenth century, leaving a pronounced mark on New England Protestantism. If it is mildly paradoxical, given Feeney's intense antipathies toward Harvard, that his community should end up in a town bearing the same name as the university, so also is it paradoxical that, however unconscious, theirs should be a kind of modern transcendentalism, transcendentalism being steeped in the Protestantism they once so abhorred. Perhaps the simple explanation is that the second St. Benedict's is virtually next door to the transcendentalist Eden that Bronson Alcott experimented with at Fruitlands and through which Isaac Hecker, founder of the Paulist Fathers, passed on his way to Catholicism. The preservation of Fruitlands as a museum could be responsible for preserving a transcendentalist influence in the area.

In any case, as in transcendentalism, life at St. Benedict's has its four major aspects: philosophical, theological, social, economic. Emphasis is on development of mind and soul, and toward this end the St. Benedict community lives a life of worship and prayer, silence, meditation and study. St. Benedict's has its own school. Many of its 146 acres are in hay and crops; chickens and a prize herd of Holsteins supply dairy and poultry products. In the transcendentalist tradition, theirs is a largely self-contained living. Days are arduous; evenings are for relaxation, and the community gathers in what the transcendentalists called "social communion." It is the time when the person who opened the Center's day with a Latin Mass closes it with reflections and an account of what is happening beyond the Center's green pastures. There is no television at St. Benedict's, no radio (except for rare occasions like elections), no newspapers. Leonard

Feeney, the font of spiritual life, becomes now the font of knolwedge, and into the community filters news of world and religion, shaped—presumably—according to the preferences of the narrator.

I visited St. Benedict Center in Still River of a December Friday in 1972, when the sky was heavy with snow and my feelings tinged with uncertainty. A journalist was entering where journalists did not tread, at least then. They were unwelcome—first because of memories of the Cambridge past, when the press frequently acted as inquisitors and prosecutors; secondly, because the St. Benedict's community had long since come to the conclusion that it had nothing to add to what had already been said. Inevitably, the response to my overtures about visiting was not enthusiastic. I could come and observe, but there would be no interviews. And there were none. A handshake and some brief words with Leonard Feeney (who, despite his then 75 years looked much better than a friend had earlier reported him to be); a superficial tour of the property; some generalized conversation with three Brothers of Feeney's religious order, who answered questions but allowed no note-taking. It was all very sociable, but at the same time eerie. Matching the experience with my research, I had the inescapable feeling of being among a community of persons bent on their own dissolution.

For at the time, St. Benedict's could only be classified as self-eliminating. No new members had been received into the religious order since 1955, and no recruits had been sought. Similarly, no children had been born to Center families for fifteen years. Thirty-nine of the community's seventy-eight members were offspring of married members of the community, but there would be no third-generation St. Benedict's family. After the move to Still River in 1958, married couples were required to separate, turn in their wedding rings, and take the same vows of chastity and celibacy as the single members. Thus, as unwillingness to recruit had shut off growth from the outside, so had policy with respect to family life arrested internal growth.

More to the point, there was on hand no priest-successor to Leonard Feeney, and this loomed as the decisive factor in the Center's future. Feeney was the community's sole link to the sacramental life, so that when he died or became incapacitated there would be no one to celebrate Mass, to consecrate the host, to hear confessions, to perform the range of priestly tasks. There was no predicting what would happen then. The Center could have collapsed, so complete was the cultic dependency on Leonard Feeney. As a banished ex-member of the community, Robert J. Colopy, commented, "They really need a priest. These people really believe. They are not frauds." There were additional factors.

A correlative psychic dependency on Leonard Feeney and the community's own ideas of orthodoxy would prevent the community from shopping around for a priest to take Feeney's place. Since no Chancery or religious order would assign a priest to the Center before a reconciliation with Rome, they perhaps would have had to settle for a priest in less than good standing. This would cut against the Center's Tridentine grain. (Feeney's own ecclesiastical standing, or lack thereof, had never been a problem for the St. Benedict's people, as at no point did they concede the legitimacy of the actions taken against him.)

If it seemed curious that a group "outside the pale" would want to play by the Establishment's rules rather than by swinging rules of its own, it was only the mildest of the curiosities encountered at St. Benedict's. This was a community where children were handed over to the group for upbringing ("Mister, are you my father," a seeking child once asked of an adult), where brother and sister did not necessarily know their relationship, where no marital or familial displays of affection were allowed. It was a community, too, where a wife would label husband "traitor" for wavering on "the doctrine," and where children would wish their father dead for the same reason.

It happened to Robert Colopy several years before, after he sought to persuade his wife to flee St. Benedict's with him and take with them their five sons. Loretta Colopy turned her husband in to the community, and Colopy was stripped of his cassock, as in disgrace, before the whole group. Everything was taken from him except his driver's license, and he was driven to the outskirts of Boston, where, penniless, he either bolted from the car or was dumped (each side has its version of the story). Colopy made his way to a police station, borrowed a dime, and made a collect call to Bishop Bernard Flanagan of Worcester, in whose diocese the Town of Harvard is located. Bishop Flanagan helped ease Colopy back into the world, and Colopy hurried into court with a suit seeking custody of his children, then approximately 8 to 14 years old. This was in the early 1960s, and the trial constituted the world's window on St. Benedict's as columns of newspaper coverage exploded the details of the Center's special way of life.

Robert Colopy won his custody suit, Judge Carl E. Wahlstrom of Worcester County Probate Court ruling that a mother's allegiance to a religious sect over marriage vows and family constituted desertion. A higher court upheld the ruling, and on January 25, 1965, the five Colopy boys were turned over to their father. "They have told me that they pray I die," Colopy remarked at one point, "but I had to get them out of there." It spoke strongly for the tug of the community, however, that five years later at least two of the Colopy boys were back at St. Benedict's and registered voters of the Town of Harvard.

It was difficult to pinpoint the element that kept the Feeney community firmly welded together after a quarter-century and that drew back children after they had reached the age of decision-making for themselves. But very probably it had something to do with what Jesuit Father Avery Dulles, a co-founder of the original St. Benedict Center, calls the working of "a collective psychology," in which loyalty to the group and loyalty to an idea are inextricably interwoven. And then, of course, there was Leonard Feeney, who, so far as the community was concerned, was loyalty personified, going back to the days in Cambridge. If anyone whom Leonard Feeney loved and trusted went out on a limb, he would climb out on the same limb. However admirable the impulse, the results were fatal for Leonard Feeney. For it led him to extremes of emotion and of position that were the undoing of a brilliant career and of an experiment which, for intellectual content and activity involving young people, was unique in Boston and maybe in American Catholicism.

St. Benedict Center began life modestly in 1940 as a gathering place for Catholics attending Harvard, Radcliffe and other nearby "secular" colleges. The Center was the idea of Mrs. Catherine Goddard Clarke, subsequently the Center's historian and until her death one of its moving spirits; Margaret Knapp, also deceased, who left St. Benedict's to join the Sisters of the Sacred Heart; and Avery Dulles, at the time a student at Harvard Law School and recent convert to Catholicism, and now the prominent Jesuit theologian.

The Center's beginnings were promising, but inconspicuous. It was Father Leonard Feeney, then at the peak of his fame as a poet, essayist and lecturer, who projected it into religious and intellectual prominence, so that by the late 1940s the Center could boast 200 converts, 100 persons influenced to become priests or nuns, and 250 students enrolled in academic courses in Greek, church history, hagiography, literature and philosophy. It was a heady time. The State accredited St. Benedict Center scholastically; the Federal Government approved it for inclusion within the G. I. Bill; the then-Archbishop of Boston, Richard Cushing, was writing articles for the Center's publication, *From the Housetops*; young Monsignor John Wright, Cushing's secretary, now a Roman cardinal, was a frequent visitor; the top Catholic lecturers came to speak. Progress was astonishing, and no one disputed the fact that credit belonged to the magical Leonard Feeney.

Leonard Feeney first came to St. Benedict's out of curiosity, as one who had heard glowing reports and wished to know more. An immediate enthusiast, Feeney began traveling frequently, then almost daily to the Center from the Jesuit seminary in Weston, where he was teaching. He would preside afternoons over tea cups, and Thursday evenings from a small rostrum in the Center's huge and invariably over-flowing main meeting room; always he was available for private consultations. St. Benedict's had no official chaplain then, and in those days of lay dependency on priests, he was the answer to many prayers. People at the Center began to press Chancery to name him as chaplain. Chancery, impressed by Feeney's volunteer ministry, did not need much persuading. He was named full-time to St. Benedict's in 1943.

Leonard Feeney was then in his mid-40s and as genuine a religious celebrity as one could find. He had a dozen books to his credit, including *In Towns and Little Towns*, which had gone through eleven printings between 1927 and 1930 alone, and *Fish on Friday*, a best seller after its appearance in 1934. Sheed & Ward was readying for the presses a *Leonard Feeney*

Omnibus, and organizations across the country were vying for his presence. The past was a succession of glorious moments, such as the preaching of the 1937 Advent sermons in St. Patrick's Cathedral, Cardinal Hayes and *Time* sitting in. ("How about a St. Barbara of Brooklyn, a St. Helen of the Bronx, and a St. Robert of Jersey City?" Feeney asked in discussing the calendar of saints. *Time* countered by proposing a St. Francis, a St. Knute and a St. Joyce, after Father Francis Duffy of the Fighting 69th Regiment, Knute Rockne and Joyce Kilmer.) For Feeney, the future seemed unlimited. It was a wonderful world for this son of Irish immigrants, the oldest of the three Feeney priest-brothers from Lynn, Mass. Leonard Feeney enjoyed his fame immensely.

For several years, the Feeney appointment was a dazzling one. His reputation glamorized the Center, and his talents complemented neatly the Center's intellectual and religious ambitions (a few said "pretensions"). At the same time, his reputation as a spiritual director grew so great that Chancery took to worrying that the physical growth of the Center would diminish the time Feeney devoted to counseling. All gifts seemed his, including the facility of striking the perfect balance between the heavy and the light, the serious and the gay. He had a delightful wit, and while not everyone was overwhelmed by his theological depth, no one lacked appreciation for his humor. An exquisite mimic, Leonard Feeney would imitate Katherine Hepburn broadcasting a Joe Louis prizefight. Audiences loved it and shouted for more. Feeney would encore with Fulton Sheen expounding in the mode of Isaiah the Prophet on the blessing that was Coca Cola ("Ho, everyone that thirsteth for the pause that refreshes . . ."), with Franklin Roosevelt declaiming on the sorry state of religion in the United States ("And in certain underprivileged parts of our country, we have only two paltry sacraments—and not one single Bingo game!"). Feeney heightened effects by having the mimicked speak on topics alien to their competencies or their interests; thus, Al Smith lecturing on scholastic philosophy and Eleanor Roosevelt broadcasting from Calvary on Good Friday.

"These were no second-rate impersonations," reminisced a Boston man who knew St. Benedict Center in 1943 and 1944 while associated with the Army Chaplains' School at Harvard. "These were priceless moments that left a person in a fit of laughter." Feeney's best imitation, he maintained, "was when he would take off his Roman collar, place it on the top of his head, and then say in a funny, squeaky voice, "I'm Mother Cabrini.' You'd almost swear he was."

Later, as tensions quickened between Feeney and religious officials, the imitations changed into frontal attacks on those he branded doctrinal liberals for not holding strict on *extra ecclesiam nulla salus*. His principal targets became Archbishop Cushing; John Wright, at this stage Auxiliary Bishop; and Father William L. Keleher, S. J., president of Boston College. The transformation worried friends. They saw the joy and characteristic good humor draining from the man, and sensed that a deeper change was taking place. An intensity was setting in that would make Leonard Feeney a totally different person. *Commonweal* executive editor John Cogley detected the shifted mood and later wrote that it was hard to realize this "angry, splenetic man" was the same individual who wrote *Fish on Friday* and the cheerful verse of *In Towns and Little Towns*.

For Leonard Feeney and the people of St. Benedict's, all the chips went on the table after the Enola Gay dumped the atomic bomb on Hiroshima in 1945. This was the apocalyptic event confirming for them the vice and corruption of the world. With Communism advancing on the one side, and, on the other, the United States stooping to the barbarism of nuclear weapons, where was there to turn but to truths beyond both? Suddenly, salvation became all-consuming, and what other salvation was there than salvation through the Catholic church?

The St. Benedict's community was not hurling down a challenge to Catholic authority when it locked onto *extra ecclesiam nulla salus*, at least not at first. It thought it was being consistent with the teaching of twenty-nine Doctors of the church, with Boniface VIII's *Unam Sanctam* ("Furthermore, We declare, say, define and pronounce, that it is wholly necessary for the salvation of every human creature to be subject to the Roman Pontiff"), with the Syllabus of Errors ("It is error to believe that men can, in the cult of any religion, find the way to eternal salvation and attain eternal salvation"), with the Profession of Faith sworn to by Pius IX and the Fathers of Vatican Council I ("This true Catholic faith, outside of which no one can be saved . . ."), with popular Catholic tradition (Weren't we all taught in parochial school that the Catholic church was the one, true church?).

Applying the doctrine with a literalness that could only lead to conflict, Leonard Feeney and the St. Benedict's community soon saw Harvard University as "a pest-hole" of atheism and Marxism; its president, James Bryant Conant was a "thirty-third degree Masonic brute." (Feeney accused Conant of once having said at a private party that the United States should have dropped ten atomic bombs on Japan "to make a more interesting experiment.") At the same time, Jesuit-operated Boston College had lapsed into "heresy" for teaching in its theology department that others than formal Catholics might achieve salvation; Archbishop Cushing was diluting Catholic interests by sitting down to dinner at Harvard's Lowell House, and Bishop Wright came under suspicion for speaking against conscription at Harvard's Liberal Union. The whole business was getting nutty.

It would have been one thing if the Feeney people had kept their resentments and their charges "within the family." But when they went public with them, "the Feeneyites" (a term of disparagement that had grown current) exploded into controversy and embarrassment. The Center by now had several people who were speaking out, but Leonard Feeney was identified as the source of all logic. The Jesuits—with the concurrence, if not encouragement of Chancery—

sought to quiet him and, failing that, ordered him to Holy Cross College in Worcester: outside the archdiocese and to hell and gone away from Harvard Square. That was in summer, 1948. Leonard Feeney refused to go. In so refusing, the issue for him was joined: he would sink or swim, be vindicated or be damned, on his interpretation of salvation doctrine. Feeney's refusal, however, also resolved a dilemma for his religious superiors. They were now able to hold Leonard Feeney in disobedience to his vows, and thus leapfrog the doctrinal question posed by him. (Feeney had been demanding a doctrinal hearing on *extra ecclesiam nulla salus*.) From that point on, the contention between Feeney and the church locally moved on ever-widening tangents.

Looking back, one is struck with the incredible swiftness with which events piled on top of one another. On May 2, 1948, Father Feeney and more than 1,200 members and friends of the Center were welcomed warmly at the Archbishop's residence. Carrying a statue of the Infant of Prague, a gift to the Center from Archbishop Josef Beran of Prague, they marched in procession about the grounds, filling the air with Marian hymns and Hail Marys. (St. Benedict Center was always and still is Mary-centered.) Archbishop Cushing greeted the group and applauded comments by Archduke Rudolph of the House of Hapsburg and Count Edmund Czernin of Prague, a member of the Center. There were happy goodbyes all around. "It was a magical afternoon," Catherine Goddard Clarke recorded in *The Loyolas and the Cabots*,

The Story of the Boston Heresy Case (Ravengate, Boston, 1950.) In reality, it was only the magical calm before the wild storm.

Within months came the silencing of Leonard Feeney; the placing of St. Benedict's under interdict; the firing of four Feeney partisans from the faculties of Boston College and Boston College High School; a condemnation from the Vatican; and, finally, the dismissal of Father Feeney from the Jesuit order. The dismissal arrived by registered mail. According to *The Loyolas and the Cabots*, Feeney "was seated in his chair, reading a book, and many of the Center students were at nearby tables, working hard at their studies." Feeney signed a Post Office receipt for Mailman Haley, and with the unopened letter still in hand, turned to the students and said, "My dear boys and girls, I have been dismissed from the Jesuit order." The date was October 28, 1949. It had been only eighteen months since the blissful day of the Infant of Prague procession.

The story of the Boston Heresy Case is not a good guys-bad guys narrative: it is much too complex for easy judgment. The establishment's side was, by general agreement, the right side; history has not dislodged that belief. On the other hand, at given stages in the contention, Leonard Feeney's positions were not without merit. Doctrinally, there was what seemed to be traditional teaching about salvation—certainly traditional enough to have entitled Feeney to the formal doctrinal hearing he wanted. Authorities were as adamant in the one direction as Feeney was in the other. Years later, Father Hans Kung would allow in a lecture at Fordham that Leonard Feeney's position on salvation doctrine was, on the surface, what the church had taught for centuries. And Avery Dulles, in his 1971 book *The Survival of Dogma* (Doubleday) would use the proposition *extra ecclesiam nulla salus* to illustrate his thesis of "reconceptualization" of dogma in Catholicism. By extending the Küng and Dulles logic—or applying it retroactively—Feeney would appear to have deserved a doctrinal hearing. What seems clear now is that the Catholic church of the 1940s was in a process of evolution, if not of dogma then of the interpretation of dogma; in not evolving too, Leonard Feeney became victim of the process.

For Feeney there were other grievances. If Catherine Clarke's account of events is only half-accurate, the order to Leonard Feeney to pack and be off to Holy Cross College was not accompanied by a fully candid explanation for the countermanding of the assignment of only a few weeks before to remain at St. Benedict's for another year. By the same token, the placing of the Center under interdict seemingly did not include the three canonical warnings to which Feeney said it was entitled. Nor was the 1949 letter from the Congregation of the Holy Office censuring Feeney and repudiating the Center's teachings on salvation made available at the time to Feeney in its entirety. (Several years later, the letter was published; by then the rumor had spread that the complete letter was withheld because it contained a rebuke to Archbishop Cushing for not taking appropriate and timely steps against St. Benedict's. The rumor appears unfounded.) There were additional lesser grievances—like the Catholic press's not verifying news about Feeney with Feeney himself; like the *American Catholic Who's Who's* expunging of him from its pages after the 1948-49 edition. Feeney was not excommunicated by Rome until February 16, 1953, but obviously it was enough then to be in disfavor to be erased as a Catholic Who's-Who.

Yet, when everything is totaled up, it was probably more than dogma alone that settled Feeney's fate. A decisive element undoubtedly was the hate that had infected thought processes and which erupted in rhetorical violence against Jews. Alongside this hate, the slurs on Protestants were virtual valentines (they with their "Mary-hating faces") and Catholic "un-friendlies" (that "weak-kneed heretic," Archbishop Cushing; that "archdiocesan ragman," a derisive reference to Cushing's scrap-newspaper fund-drives).

The anti-Semitism of the Feeney people reached a peak after Feeney took his witness to the Boston Common around 1950. Feeney and his followers would march sullen and unsmiling onto the Charles Street Mall, behind a banner of Our Lady and a crucifix; set up a podium, sing hymns, then launch into what *Life* magazine labeled "wild and inflammatory speeches." Much of the denunciation of Jews was done by a William Smith, a Feeney disciple from Harvard, but when the heckling grew heated, Feeney would join in with shouts about "filthy demons" and "frauds," and the Common's being "circumcision circle." "I hate anyone who likes the Jews," he is quoted as once saying. "People who like the Jews are loudmouthed and stupid like Archbishop Cushing." The shouts grew sick and irrational. "They hate the water of baptism!" an Anti-Defamation League bulletin of B'nai B'rith recorded Feeney as saying, "I hate you—a dirty rotten face like that! You dogs! Go home! I will ask the Blessed Virgin to punish you!"

It was sad and pathetic to Cathlics; to Jews, it was understandably worrisome. It was, after all, only a few years since the holocaust, and what assurances were there that what had happened in Germany would not happen again elsewhere? Jewish organizations strenuously protested Feeney's anti-Semitism to civil and religious authorities. Meanwhile, individual Jews traveled to Boston Common in an effort to counter the hate. "I can remember carloads of young Jews, from Brandeis, from Dorchester, loading up on Sunday afternoons to go and hassle Feeney," Mark Mirsky recalled in the December, 1971, issue of *Metro*, a Boston publication. "We were all reeling from the holocaust, and Feeney looked like a little Hitler to us. We wanted to stop him now, when he was small, and not take the chance."

As Leonard Feeney refused to be silenced by church authorities, so on Boston Common did he refuse to be outhassled by his audiences. Sunday by Sunday the spectacle grew more tense, until police, fearful of a riot, approached Mayor John Hynes on closing off Boston Common to the Feeney group. Mayor Hynes declined to interfere, holding that soapbox orators, however unsavory, had a right to use the grounds. In effect the decision was to let the Feeney people talk themselves out—which they did, but not quickly and not before scarring many innocent parties.

There is no rational explanation for Feeney's anti-Semitic passions of those years. There were occasional infelicities toward Jews in earlier writings of the type common among Catholics in the decades before Vatican II's Declaration on the Jews, but no clue to what was to come. It was an incredible progression from the 1935 rhymes of "Epiphany" ("Now the King-less Jews, I guess,/ Are checkmated,/ And their little game of chess/ Terminated./ Two white kings and one black/ The Gentiles used in their attack.") . . . to the crudities of *London Is a Place* ("One may ask who is responsible for what is known as the London Jew?") . . . to the slanders of *The Point*, successor to *From the Housetops* ("From the time the Apostles first began to evangelize nations, the Catholic church has had one great, fierce, and enduring enemy. That enemy is the Jews . . .") . . . to the ravings of the Boston Common ("You, you hooknosed Jew, what have you to say?").

By the same token, there is no rational explanation for the roughhouse and violence that became a part of the Center's encounters. Certainly Leonard Feeney did not inspire either by his own physique. A small man, he was quite slight until later years added weight. He could be given to towering rages (Robert Colopy claims that Feeney once slapped him, shattering his glasses), but he was also known in his earlier years as a gentle man. There was nothing gentle, however, in many of his followers: the brawny McIsaac brothers, Feeney's "bodyguards," one of whom would leap to the platform after Feeney finished a Sunday tirade, warning that anyone trying to hurt Feeney would have to do so over his dead body; or the twenty-five who stormed the Washington residence of the Apostolic Delegate in 1952 demanding justice for Father Feeney (they were hauled away by police); or the six who were hurried off the Notre Dame campus allegedly for attempting to incite a riot ("The first sign of your approaching damnation," shouted one, "is that Notre Dame has Protestants on its football team"); or the three who trashed Msgr. Francis Lally's editor's office at the Boston *Pilot* in 1955 (because Lally was associating with "Christ-killers"ʰ and "heretics"). If Leonard Feeney did nothing to encourage this aggressiveness— and other less muscular exercises in the pushing of the Center's books and pamphlets—he also did nothing about disowning it.

But the largest puzzle, and ultimately the crucial one, remained Leonard Feeney's cementing of himself in the *extra ecclesiam nulla salus* thing. The paradox is that Feeney was not always a hard-liner on salvation. In *Fish on Friday*, for instance, he provided reflectively for the salvation of two YWCA train-companions (". . . for God loves us for our efforts and forgives us our ignorances"). Under whatever influences, his reasoning began to change during his early years at St.

Benedict's. "His position would take different forms based on his various moods," Avery Dulles reminisced to me one day in New York. "If he was in an optimistic mood, he would be possessed with the mercy of God that everything was love and forgiveness. If he was in a severe mood, then nobody got salvation except those in the Catholic church." Dulles accounts for the variations of mood by Feeney's poetic nature. "You've got to remember that Leonard Feeney was a poet," he declared, "and like all poets his mood affected very much what he was saying." Eventually Feeney settled into the severe mold.

One element that very likely helped fix Feeney in his hard doctrinal position on salvation was his special concept of loyalty to those he had converted to Catholicism or caught up in his salvation logic. Many had sacrificed much by casting their lot with Leonard Feeney, and he was not about to turn his back on them or tell them their stand was an erroneous one. Temple Morgan, for one. Porcellian Club, captain of the Harvard boxing team, scion of one of Harvard's most prominent families (his grandfather had given Harvard one of its gates); how do you tell "Temp" that he need not have resigned Harvard on a point of religious principle (just a few months before graduation), that he need not have spurned the advice of family, that there were, after all, avenues of salvation other than through baptism by water and allegiance to the Pope? How do you tell Fakhri Maluf, assistant professor of philosophy, Boston College; James R. Walsh, instructor in philosophy, Boston College; Charles Ewaskio,

assistant professor of physics, Boston College; David
D. Supple, instructor of German, Boston College High
School—how do you tell them that they were fired in
vain, that *extra ecclesiam nulla salus* suddenly meant
something more than what they had held? You do not,
if yours was the loyalty of Leonard Feeney. Feeney
hung solid, thus making his a mistake of the heart as
well as the mind.

But mistakes were made on the other side as well. It
seems a mistake, for one thing, not to have given
Feeney the doctrinal hearing he desired, or at least to
have thrown open the salvation topic to the theological
community for debate. The church risked little, for
there appears small doubt but that the consensus
emerging from such a discussion would have been
consistent with the then official position, as well as
with what emerged later from Vatican Council II—
that there is indeed salvation outside the Catholic
church. (At the time, the official church position, as
expressed in the Holy Office's 1949 letter to Archbishop Cushing, allowed for the salvation of non-
Catholics in "invincible ignorance" and those united
to the church "by desire and longing.")

Likewise, it seems a mistake to have formalized the
excommunication of Leonard Feeney. (The Holy
Office declared in its 1953 decree that Feeney
"automatically incurred excommunication" by displaying "stubborn disobedience to an order" enjoining
him to appear in Rome "before the authorities of the
Sacred Congregation.") However much patience,
charity and the "rules" had been abused, the pro-

nouncement of excommunication seems superfluous, coming as it did on top of the silencing, the withdrawal of faculties, interdiction of St. Benedict Center, and other measures. This was over-kill. The church's disapproval of Feeney and his doctrine was more than apparent. A more sensitive reading of the situation, particularly after 1949, should have suggested referral of the Feeney case to others than to excommunicators. Under the circumstances, the excommunication was excessive.

At the time of my visit to St. Benedict Center in 1972, the question was, what could be done to redeem the past? The problem was tricky, but it did not seem to be insuperable. Most of the major obstacles to a reconciliation had dissipated. The hates were behind the St. Benedict's community—"We have mellowed," one of the Brothers of Feeney's order said to me. Indeed they had. Hostilities to "outsiders" had also eased markedly. In fact, one of Feeney's favorite times had come to be the party given occasionally for neighbors. At these, Feeney would be the center of the gaiety, "beaming and twinkling" and slapping on the head of those to whom he had taken a fancy an old Al Smith derby, a gift from the great man himself. St. Benedict Center, in a word, had ceased to be the ecumenical embarrassment it once was. The Center lagged liturgically and doctrinally, but that seemed no special problem. I recall feeling that the Center's hyperorthodoxy would have a strong nostalgic appeal in many Roman quarters.

To me, the community appeared to ache quietly for reconciliation, and the only question was how reconciliation would come about. Certainly Leonard Feeney and the St. Benedict community would not turn and fall on their knees to Rome—go to Canossa, so to speak. The initiative, I thought, would have to come from outside the Center and be very subtle.

Father Avery Dulles commented in our little talk that "there must be a way by which the excommunication can be lifted without their having to make a formal retraction, and without the church seeming to accept their position." His was a wistful thought, but, as it turned out, a prophetic one.

Within two years—following discreet interventions by Bishop Flanagan, Cardinal Humberto Medeiros of Boston, and Cardinal John Wright, by now of the Vatican's Congregation for the Clergy—the Feeney excommunication and other sanctions were lifted by Pope Paul VI. In March of 1974, twenty-nine members of the community made a "simple profession of faith" before Bishop Flanagan, and for them the ordeal with Rome was over. No recantation was demanded; they were not required to disavow their former ideas on salvation. For the twenty-nine, the action was no cave-in; as one Brother rationalized, there is more room for disparity of opinion and more latitude for discussion in the church today. The group formed a new community known as the Pious Union of Benedictine Oblates of Still River, and started about the ecclesiastical process by which members could develop into a canonically-recognized religious institute of the Order of St. Benedict. Ultimately they hope to become a Benedictine priory or abbey. This group has roughly twenty-six male and nineteen female members, as well as some members who do not live at the house but participate in prayer, study and work according to the Benedictine tradition. In December, 1976, two members of the group were ordained to the priesthood—one according to the Latin Rite; the other, the Maronite Catholic Rite—thus settling worries about the community's sacramental future after the death of Leonard Feeney. The ordinations came none too soon. Within fourteen months, Leonard Feeney was dead and in a grave on St. Benedict's grounds.

The Boston Heresy Case, accordingly, has its happy ending—almost, that is. Eighteen members of St. Benedict Center refused to make the 1974 "simple profession of faith," maintaining that their orthodoxy made even the most perfunctory of gestures unnecessary and humiliating. They split from the larger group and took up residence in another building on the St. Benedict's property. There has been little contact since between the two groups, other than the sharing of priest and kitchen—as one might say: food for the soul, and food for the body.

AFTERWORD: That splinter group has undergone further splintering over recent months, and a legal battle has developed over riches and property. Feeney, in trust and indiscretion, years ago placed ownership of the St. Benedict's property in the names of all members of the community, thus making it possible for latter-day challenges from splinter groups for their share of the whole. A privately arranged legal division was being arranged the last I heard, and there could be three or as many as four subdivisions of the original St. Benedict's before matters are finally settled. One report has the ultra-conservative John Birch Society supporting one of the splinter groups, and a chapel being planned for the celebration of the proscribed Tridentine Mass.

V

JOHN COURTNEY MURRAY

The Jesuit from Olympus

IN HIS MOST INFLUENTIAL DAYS, Father John
Courtney Murray, S. J., was by most popular yardsticks a relatively anonymous person. His writing
appeared for the most part in esoteric or specialized
journals of limited circulation. His campus presence,
except for a brief period as a visiting professor of
philosophy at Yale, was confined pretty much to a
seminary in rural Maryland. He moved in the councils
of the mighty—the intellectually mighty—but not
conspicuously so far as publicity and renown were
concerned. Even at Vatican Council II, an event which
he helped give its decisive shape, John Courtney
Murray moved behind the scenes, a non-voting figure
shunning the spotlight of public debate and the plat-
forms of propagandists. He was there for three
sessions. Our times overlapped; I didn't see him once
at press briefings or public musters, and my experience was that of others. As an actor on the stage of
history, John Courtney Murray needed no periodic
excursions into the limelight, no plaudits, no curtain
calls. The performance was what counted; more
particularly, the results. He performed superbly; the
results were large.

Thus the inevitability of what Jesuit Father Walter
J. Burghardt foresaw at Murray's funeral Mass in

1967: "Unborn millions will never know how much their freedom is tied to this man . . . how much the civilized dialogue they take for granted between Christian and Christian, between Christian and Jew, between Christian and unbeliever was made possible by this man, whose life was a civilized conversation." They don't, just as, as Burghardt also remarked, untold numbers of American Catholics do not appreciate how much more gracefully they live as Americans and as Catholics precisely because of this reticent Jesuit who lives beyond death as the most perceptive definer of the American Proposition and one of the most effective secular and religious ecumenists of the twentieth century.

John Courtney Murray's life was indeed the personification of civilized dialogue: intelligent, rational, deliberate, gentlemanly. More importantly, it led somewhere, unlike so much dialogue, civilized or not, which wastes itself on the air around it. On one level John Courtney Murray helped lay to rest the last of the nativist bromides about Catholic incompatibility to a democratic America because of alleged first-loyalties to Rome. On another, he helped disperse within Catholicism itself ancient ambiguities about personal freedom, as well as the institutional double-speak by which Catholicism claimed freedom where Catholics were a minority, privilege where they were a majority.

Murray's accomplishments were measurable in the concrete. Americans elected their first Catholic President in 1960, and John Courtney Murray was sufficiently responsible for the change in climate that made the impossible possible for John Fitzgerald Kennedy. Before the crucial appearance of the candidate at the inquisition of the Houston Ministerial Association, the candidate's comments on Church and State were cleared for exactness with Murray by telephone.* Later would come Vatican II, and the landmark Declaration on Religious Freedom. The bishops—the Council Fathers—voted the Declaration, and the Pope, Paul VI, promulgated it. But no one was more responsible for the thrust of the Declaration, its very words, than John Courtney Murray.

By extension, the Declaration on Religious Freedom would generate in the decade after the Council momentous expressions of individual freedom within institutional Catholicism—on moral questions, such as birth control, divorce, second marriages, to cite no others; and in the area of discipline, as for instance whether priests and religious were to remain virtual serfs of bishops and superiors, or whether they were to be allowed freedoms of their own according to the implicit if not express meaning of the Declaration.

* The telephone call is cited by the caller, Theodore C. Sorensen, later Special Counsel to President Kennedy, in his book *Kennedy* [Harper & Row, 1965]. Sorensen said the wish was to avoid "any loose wording . . . that would stir up the Catholic press," the Catholic press hawking Kennedy as much in the one direction as the Texas ministers were in the other. Murray would later say that he may have suggested some changes, but couldn't remember what they were. He recalled, however, being annoyed that he should have been asked opinion and advice "just on hearing the speech on the phone."

That some expressions of freedom may have carried beyond the bounds of propriety is less important than that they suddenly were possible at all . . . and at long last. More broadly, the placement of the individual conscience over the letter of rule and regulation, a primary development of the Declaration, made it possible for the Catholic church to remain "home" for thousands upon thousands who hitherto would have withdrawn or been ostracized, anathematized, hounded out of the church for some transgression against practice, custom or decorum. These Catholics could "stay" in good conscience, if not always with the good wishes of authority figures. The church would be a more humane, and human institution.

Unhappily, John Courtney Murray would not be on hand to help resolve the tensions that quickened within the church with the Declaration and the new freedoms. He died a too early death, at age 63. More sadly, there would be no one to take his place. John Courtney Murray was a unique man, a man with a particular expertise for an especially challenging moment of secular and ecclesiastical history. When he was gone, there was no one else.

John Courtney Murray's special gift, in the words of columnist John Cogley, was to combine two venerable traditions in one person, the ancient Catholic tradition of reasoned argument and the American tradition of free debate. It was a felicitous combination for the American Church as well as the American State, partly because of the tenaciousness with which old questions about Catholicism's place in the American experiment had dogged country and citizen; partly, too, because of the narrow and abrasive ways with which Catholics frequently responded to the impugning of their place in American society. Until Murray happened along, there had been, in Cogley's words, "a tendency among Catholic thinkers, wise in the ways of logic, to brush aside the special pragmatic needs of American society and concentrate on resounding moral pronunciamento, the naked absolute," while at the same time there had been "a general tendency in American life to by-pass reason in national controversy in favor of emotion, slogan, group prejudice and wit." Murray was instrumental in changing things by bringing calm and substance to the public debate, and a large measure of mutual trust.

It was—lest memories be short—a testy time. It was the period of Paul Blanshard, and therefore of wild accusation and intemperate name-calling, of mockery . . . and of Catholic reaction that often was hardly a cut above the provocations. Murray had the wisdom to see that the "New Nativism" directed against Catholics was not, as many Catholics thought, Protestant in its origins, but secular or naturalist. Likewise, he recognized that the framing of arguments in contexts that invoked Americanist and "un-American" slogans signaled a singularly dangerous cultural and patriotic trend. He argued his point with his pen, and the rejoinders to Blanshard in *The Month* (April, 1951) and to more reputable disputants like Dean Walter Russell Bowie of Union Theological Seminary in

American Mercury [September, 1949] made Murray something of an intellectual folk-hero among people of whatever persuasion. Murray's logic outreached allegiances and loyalties, prejudices and subjectivities, and staked out a future where Church and State could coexist separately and confidently, one with the other, free of old suspicions rooted in alleged prerogatives and presumed priorities. Inevitably, large minds and prominent personalities were attracted to Murray, one being Henry R. Luce of the *Time-Life* publishing empire. Luce esteemed Murray as his "closest Catholic friend," relaxed with him—and probably used him, as he was known to use others. W. A. Swanberg, for instance, reports in his book *Luce and His Empire* (Scribner's, 1972) that "Lucepress" editors were less sure that the Murray-Luce association was a friendship in the usual sense than an endless series of intellectual duels about religious and social abstractions between two men who enjoyed dueling." From this swordplay, Luce is characterized as coming out with new thrusts to try on the editors. The observation would seem to indicate that the friendship might have had more bearing on Luce than it did on Murray. But whether it did or did not is not particularly important. One is grateful that Murray escaped Luce's politics . . . and his prose style . . . and any disastrous consequences from some dangerous experimentation with the hallucinogenic drug LSD. Luce was an early enthusiast for LSD, having taken the drug, according to Swanberg, under the guidance of Dr. Sidney Cohen of Los Angeles. Clare Boothe Luce, Henry Luce's wife, also joined in LSD "trips," and like her husband allegedly experienced new levels of appreciation for the sights and sounds around them. Murray is reported to have gone along on one of the "trips," apparently to experience the drug's mind-expansion effects. Swanberg writes that the Luces "were fortunate in having had no bad trips." The same seems to have been true of Murray.

What was he like, this Murray? He was tall, slim, bespectacled, a deadly serious man—cerebral and intellectually intimidating. He did not suffer fools gladly. Yet he was human enough to enjoy a game of golf, and to want his Beefeater martinis "desperately dry." It is said, too, that he made a "mean stinger." But don't get the idea that Murray was a drinker. He wasn't.

He was a native New Yorker, his earliest days lived in the 19th Street area, when this was a quite fashionable part of town. His mother was Irish, his father Scots. According to Murray, the father was a born Catholic who "strayed" in his youth but "rallied around" after marriage.

John Courtney Murray was born September 12, 1904. He did his growing up in Jamaica, in the Borough of Queens, and thought for a time of becoming a lawyer like his father. Instead he joined the Society of Jesus at age 16, and traveled a not unfamiliar Jesuit route: B.A. from Weston College in Massachusetts in 1926, M.A. from Boston College in 1927, regency in the Philippines, theology and ordination [June 25, 1933] at Woodstock College in Maryland, doctoral studies at the Gregorian University in Rome. Murray did his dissertation on Matthias Scheeben's doctrine of supernatural divine faith, and was awarded his doctorate in 1937. He thereupon joined the faculty at Woodstock as a professor of theology, handling courses in grace and the Trinity.

As a professor, Murray belonged to the old school. His lectures were formal and "almost Olympian in manner," according to Father Leo J. O'Donovan, S. J., of the Weston School of Theology in Cambridge, Massachusetts. O'Donovan studied the Trinity under Murray in 1965-66, after the Council, when Murray's fatigued body was wearing towards its last. By this time Murray was an Olympian figure himself, particularly to young Jesuits like O'Donovan, and he fit their Olympian impressions. "His lectures were not impersonal or distant," O'Donovan recalled recently, "but they *were* lectures, declaimed and very imposing. He allowed time for discussion, but discussion periods were not his preferred mode of teaching." In some ways, O'Donovan preferred the Murray he knew from the offices of *Theological Studies*, the quarterly that Murray sired and edited, and where O'Donovan interned as a scholastic. Here the man who was solemn and stately in the classroom was warm and enjoyable, approachable ever, and at the center of the journal's socials.

Yet if the classroom manner left something to be desired, the intellectual content did not. Nor the man

himself. More than twenty Woodstock ordination
classes, including O'Donovan's, selected Father John
Courtney Murray to give their ordination retreat. That
he should have been asked so often, and that he should
have been so often available, speaks worlds about the
man, his personal spirituality, and his interest in new
generations of Jesuits. "For they were grueling, those
retreats," O'Donovan commented. "Four conferences
a day, along with being available for individual
conferences, for eight days running."

To some, John Courtney Murray seemed aloof, but
those who knew him intimately, like Walter Burghardt, realized that this supposed aloofness was
really shyness, terrible shyness. Murray was gentle,
said Burghardt, "as only the strong tested by fire can
be gentle." He was courteous, he was open. And for a
person of such towering intellect, he was remarkably
subservient—in the traditional religious understand-
ing of the word—to superiors.

Catholic historian Father John Tracy Ellis once
cited Murray along with John Henry Newman,
Thomas Merton and Teilhard de Chardin as "sons of
obedience"—in other words, men who exemplified
"what Henri de Lubac had in mind when he stated
that the 'man of the Church' should speak out and
enunciate his diverse opinions, indeed, even to the
point of heroism as against the opposition of his
adversaries and superiors, but he must remember that
the 'last word is not his.' " The comment may ring
today of pietism and subservience, nevertheless it is an

accurate reflection of a facet of Murray's character. He would stand up against the keenest and toughest minds of the Church, and hold his positions rigorously. But when those to whom Murray "owed" obedience and deference spoke, he let go. Thus one finds in Murray's correspondence with superiors concessions and pleas such as these:

> "I don't want to argue with your decision [against leading a group of students to Europe in 1946, at Archbishop Cushing's request to attend youth assemblies], nor even to inquire into the reasons for it. . . . I made a mistake, I see that with quite horrible clarity. As I see that all my life I shall be, quite properly, a sucker for an idea. And also, quite probably, too inclined to take personal initiatives."

Again:

> "I really think I need a new job and a new start! I say this from a personal standpoint, thinking of what *I* think would be good for me. Knowing, of course, that one is not the ultimate judge of one's usefulness, etc., etc. [It was 1947 and Murray was seeking to resign an editorship so as to join the graduate-student faculty at Fordham University.] I want to be a student (and there might be an advantage in having a student over students). And I want to write (my main 'want'); and I want to do a bit of teaching (but not here)*. And I want an opportunity to further an interest into which half a dozen things I have done and thought about have led me—the furtherance of the lay intellectual apostolate among graduate students. In fine, I want to stay in my field, but get out of my rut! There you have it. . . . I

* Woodstock College, Maryland

have spoken my little piece! And feel the better for it, whatever happens, or whether nothing happens."

The tone of those letters notwithstanding, Murray was not obsequious. He had rather a heightened sense of the obedience, the soldierly obedience, that was the mark of the loyal Jesuit, more so in his time than now. He obeyed, even when it hurt. As he did not go to Europe, as he wished to in 1946, so he did not get the new job and new start sought in 1947. And as he was disposed to obey his superiors' judgment on those matters, so a decade later would he be disposed to accept a superior's advisory to pigeonhole a sensitive article on Church-State relations and go to "the sidelines," away from the action involving that controversial topic. Happily the superior's advice became academic almost immediately. The year was now 1958 and within a few months Pius XII would be dead, John XXIII would be reigning, and an entirely new spirit of openness would infuse the Church. John's time was a time ready-made for Murray, and he would make the most of it, turning seeming failure into vindication and acceptance.

For few would the triumph be clearer than it was for John Courtney Murray. John Henry Newman became a cardinal and one of the most respected men of Church history, but the great dreams of his life went unrealized. Merton died tragically and prematurely, cut short of his new visions. Teilhard, for all the glamour and esteem connected with his name and work, died in a Manhattan "exile" and is yet regarded suspiciously in official circles as a man of dubious orthodoxy. Of Ellis's four "sons of obedience," only Murray would be vindicated by a General Council of the Church. More deliciously for Murray, he himself would be the key instrument in that vindication. Galileo didn't fare so well. Nor did Copernicus. Nor Joan of Arc. Murray lived to see his rehabilitation and acceptance.

If the comparisons seem extravagant, it may only be because history has failed to provide full perspective on the challenge and virtually single-handed manner in which Murray met it. It may also be because in the final stages many others took up the fight he had fought much alone, including, at Vatican II, prelates who once looked on Murray as heretic and adversary. Vatican II's Declaration on Religious Freedom was, of course, Murray's signal triumph, more than twenty-three hundred bishops ultimately voting for it—and, through it, him. But Murray, in characteristic modesty, reduced his own great moment, thus contributing perhaps to the happenstance that his name never became a household word. The achievement of the Declaration, he would state, "was simply to bring the church abreast of the developments that have occurred in the secular world." In a sense the statement was true, but it was unduly self-deprecatory and it failed to take into account the Declaration's evolving additional dimension in updating the Church and its notions of freedom.

John Courtney Murray approached the universal religious freedom issue through the American Church-State question. Against the weight of centuries of Church tradition, Murray held not only that Church and State could be separate, but also that in separateness resided greater freedom and fuller theological health for the Church itself, particularly in the pluralistic State that guaranteed freedom of religion. This was hardly a congenial notion to Rome when Murray began broaching it in the mid-1940s. Though it suppressed the old labels and terminologies, Rome was still committed to those articles of the Syllabus of Errors and the condemnations of Modernism that opposed a general separation of Church and State. Rome was happy to accept American dollars and its military shield against Communism, but its Constitution was seen as no new *creed.* Mighty factions of the Church held strongly that a conjoining of Church and State, preferably along the Spanish model, was the ideal to be promoted, such a conjoining being seen, however presumptuously, as a bulwark against indifferentism, theological dilution, secularism and other unearthly evils. The principal spokesmen in the United States for this point of view were Father Joseph C. Fenton, editor of the *American Ecclesiastical Review;* Father Francis J. Connell, C.SS.R., of the Catholic University of America and first president of the Catholic Theological Society of America; and Father George W. Shea of Immaculate Conception Seminary in Darlington, New Jersey. Their anchor in Rome was the indomitable Secretary of the Holy Office, the very symbol of conservatism in the modern Church, Cardinal Alfredo Ottaviani.*

The Church-State controversy took shape in the United States with Murray's 1945 and 1946 articles in *Theological Studies,* and coalesced with Murray papers at the 1947 and 1948 conventions of the Catholic Theological Society. Murray was ill on the occasion of the 1947 meeting, and ironically his paper was read for him by the person who was to emerge as his most unrelenting antagonist. This was Fenton. Murray's probings at this point were quite cautious and politic, and Fenton was not playing himself the fool by reading Murray's paper before the Society. Fenton recognized Murray's "divergent" attitudes early on, and in reading his paper entered a codicil to the effect that "it will ultimately have been advantageous to the Society to have heard two approaches" to the theology of Church and State. Murray delivered his own paper at the 1948 meeting, and the rejoinder this time was more pointed. It came from Connell, who charged Murray with theories that were "out of harmony with the traditional belief and attitude of the Church for many centuries."

The issue was still not joined, however. Murray was more directly engaged in the "New Nativism" dispute,

* The conservative position of Church and State, anachronistic as it had been for a half-century or more by the mid-1940s, still managed to attract other than ideological reactionaries. One supporter of the Catholic traditionalist position was Monsignor John A. Ryan (1869-1945), the noted social-justice priest and labor progressive.

primarily, as noted, with Blanshard and Bowie. Then, from September, 1951, until June, 1952, was his time at Yale. The Yale assignment carried Murray away from old associates and familiar tramping grounds, but not old concerns. As Father Donald E. Pelotte, S.S.S., was to note in his book *John Courtney Murray: Theologian in Conflict* (Paulist Press, 1976), the assignment provided the occasion to pursue and deepen his interests on Church-State questions. Thus, after returning to Woodstock, Murray would begin what Pelotte describes as his "systematic formulation and defense of his position."

Murray's primary outlet almost inevitably was his own journal, *Theological Studies.* His intellectual framework was the thought of Leo XIII, as he felt he perceived it. His model was the American Proposition, the democracy of the people, the fact of a pluralistic world, and the obligation to serve the common good as distinct from the narrower good of any one group or faction. He argued calmly and persuasively, but not without consequences. To come his way were the vitriol of Fenton, rebukes from the Holy Office, an admonition to clear all writings on Church and State with Jesuit headquarters in Rome, and finally the directive of August 5, 1958, to get to the "sidelines." The directive was from the American assistant at the Jesuit Generalate in Rome, Father Vincent McCormick, S.J.

As contention built to showdown, lesser combatants peeled away until in the United States just Fenton stood tall among the opposition. He was a monsignor by now, and someone to be reckoned with. In 1955, for instance, John Tracy Ellis would be denied permission to speak in Rome on the subject "The Catholic Church and Church-State Relations in the United States" by none other than the Archbishop of Washington, Patrick O'Boyle; the Archbishop (later Cardinal) "was fearful of how Monsignor Fenton would react were he to learn" that he, O'Boyle, had extended permission to Ellis to deliver the lecture. What had made Fenton so intimidating, of course, was his theological and ideological kinship with the man who was firing the same musketry from the Holy Office in Rome that Fenton was from the *American Ecclesiastical Review* in Washington. Ottaviani, of course. Murray, in the meantime, might have been convinced that his thought was consistent with that of Leo XIII and, more particularly, that of the reigning Pius XII. Leo was long dead, however, and Pius was forever ambiguous, so that Fenton could appropriate him almost as easily as Murray could invoke him. In any case, between the historicity of Leo, the ambiguity of Pius, the strength of Ottaviani, and the persistence of Fenton, Murray's ground was slipping beneath him. So was his health. In April, 1953, Murray, not yet 50, was hospitalized for cardiac insufficiency. After that life would be as precarious for him as had been his intellectual involvements.

No single event did more to shore up Murray's spirit, his world, than the election of John XXIII to the papacy. In the new Johannine openness, Murray could return to old interests—even reassemble his personal library, which in 1955 he had "purified" of all volumes on Church and State as a "symbol of retirement." He could also reactivate a project that was to have major impact on Church and country, a project long in mind but dropped with seeming finality in 1955 after his "silencing." This was the book that would explore "the content, the foundations, the mode of formation, the validity" of the American Proposition—"at once doctrinal and practical, a theorem and a problem"—that all men are created equal; that certain truths are self-evident; that they must be held, assented to, consented to, worked into the texture of institutions, if persons are to live together in dignity, peace, unity, justice, well-being, freedom; that civil questions have their religious dimensions and that "freedom of religion" had its secular as well as denominational context. The book arrived on book stands in 1960 under the title, *We Hold These Truths, Catholic Reflections on the American Proposition,* and was hailed by the *New York Times* as "probably the most significant statement on American democracy ever published." Murray discussed civilization in the pluralistic society, taking up such questions as the response of the free world to the Soviet Communist challenge, the relevance of natural-law thinking in an increasingly relativist society, the question of Christianity and human values, censorship, religious integrity, and the future of freedom. The book was a startling success, and Murray was propelled to the cover of *Time*—the December 12, 1960, issue. (It didn't hurt to know Henry Luce after all.) *We Hold These Truths*, and the public response to it, marked the beginning of Murray's rehabilitation. Full vindication would come with Vatican II. But meanwhile there were the reviews to be savored.

Harper's delighted in the book's "sheer intellectual elegance." The *Yale Review* saw Murray generating light "where heat has been the rule." The *Saturday Review* welcomed his book as "a masterpiece of candid and lucid exposition" that asked and answered questions of the highest relevance to the American, Western and Christian situations. *The Critic* and *Commonweal* applied historical and personalist yardsticks. Daniel Callahan wrote in *Commonweal* that "whatever the final judgment of history, there can be no doubt that Murray's theological work represents the most profound attempt yet made to establish the compatability of American pluralism and Catholicism." With equal astuteness *Critic* reviewer Thomas P. Neill remarked, "Every once in a while, a single person is able to change a community's way of thinking about a subject. Such a person is John Courtney Murray, S.J., who has changed the American Catholic community's thinking about the structure and problems of Church-State relations in this country." George N. Shuster predicted in *America*, the Jesuit journal Murray once served as religion editor, that the book "will for a long time mark the place in the development of American Catholic thinking about the social order at which this thinking came of age."

We Hold These Truths was pure, vintage Murray, of course. But a tip of the biretta was due also to Sheed & Ward book editor Philip Scharper. For when Murray was suddenly free to do his book, there was now neither the time nor the stamina necessary for the preparation of a new and different manuscript. Scharper took over, searching out articles and lecture manuscripts of Murray's, looking for those which fit into an organic whole. He settled on pieces that appeared in *Religious Education, America, Social Order, Modern Age, The Critic* and *Theological Studies*, on papers delivered at seminars of The Fund for the Republic, the College of New Rochelle and Marquette University, and on Murray essays that appeared in two anthologies. Scharper arranged them and showed them to Murray, who was surprised and pleased—surprised that what he had written and said over the years in so many disparate places hung together so neatly; pleased that Scharper should have had such a professional eye for their intellectual thread. The book moved ahead. Several months later, when the project had advanced to the page-proof stage, Scharper asked Murray to whom he wished to dedicate his book. "To you, Phil," said Murray. Scharper pointed out that a dedication to an editor "would be rather unusual and misplaced." Well then, responded Murray, "I guess to no one." And so it was.

Two years later—1962—Vatican Council II opened in Rome, and bishops arrived from all over the world with their *periti*, experts, who would be available for consultation with any of the Council fathers. The American *periti* were ten, all priests: Fenton, of course, Francis J. Brennan, William J. Doheny, John Steinmueller, Rudolph Bandas, George Higgins, John Quinn, Frederick McManus, Ulric Beste and Edward Heston. Conspicuous by its absence was the name of John Courtney Murray. Originally Murray was slated to be a *peritus*, but old biases die hard in Rome and memories are long of feelings wronged and toes trod upon. Murray was "disinvited" by the Apostolic Delegate to the United States, Archbishop (later Cardinal) Egidio Vagnozzi—the very same who would be behind the banning of Murray and three other distinguished theologians from a student-sponsored lecture series at the Catholic University of America the next year*. Vagnozzi could have been acting on his own, but as a creature of the Roman Curia and stalwart conservative, he more likely was acting to implement the wishes, however indirectly perceived, of Ottaviani. John XXIII was reigning, but for many in and of Rome, John was a temporary aberration; for them, it was not a care-taker Pope, but powerful traditionalists like Ottaviani who represented the Church's future, just as they had dominated its past.

---

* The others banned were Godfrey Dieckmann, O.S.B., Father Hans Küng, Father Gustave Weigel, S.J. Vagnozzi's hand in the banning was generally conceded, though, in those days of journalistic restraint, only timidly suggested, at least in the Catholic Press. A notable exception were the articles of Father John Hugo in the *Steubenville* (Ohio) *Register*.

In any case, Murray stayed home, a deeply disappointed man. As he was to say to John Cogley, "This sort of clambake only takes place once in a man's lifetime, if he is lucky. I would hate to miss it."

That he was not permanently left out resulted from the emergence of religious liberty as the so-called American issue of Vatican II and Spellman's keen recognition of a change of time and ideological tides in the Church. Spellman, accordingly, would return to the Council's second session in 1963 with the man who personified the American idea of adjustment and change as these related to religious freedom. He would return with John Courtney Murray.

That Murray would be able to play a full and influential role in the Council hinged on his presence at the critical meeting November 11, 1963, of the full theological commission, which, under the presidency of Ottaviani, had claimed the right to review the Secretariat text on religious freedom. There's some confusion as to how Murray got to be at that meeting. Some days after November 11, he told the rector of Woodstock, Father Michael F. Maher, S.J., that he was present at the invitation of Cardinal Emile Leger of Montreal; some years after—in 1967, in fact, in a telegram expressing regrets that he could not be at Murray's funeral—then-Bishop John J. Wright of Pittsburgh indicated that Murray was present at Wright's request. Whoever got him there, it was Wright who called for his recognition, a bold stroke and a Council turning point all its own. (Xavier Rynne is mistaken in saying that it was Bishop Andre Charue of Belgium who asked Murray to speak.) *America* magazine for November 30, 1963, records what happened next:

"The president of the commission, Cardinal Ottaviani, is almost blind. He did not recognize or distinguish the tall figure of Father Murray when he spoke . . . before the Commission's members and consultants. Cardinal Ottaviani . . . leaned over to his neighbor, Cardinal Leger, to ask who was speaking. The Canadian cardinal, perhaps to spare Father Murray any unwelcome publicity at that point, replied simply: '*peritus quidam*' (one of the experts)."

I was in Rome in those heady days, and later that November 11 night met Wright at the Rome Hilton, where he had gone after the theological commission session to sit in on what remained of the annual meeting of the American Hierarchy. (During the Council years, those meetings were held in Rome.) Over fifteen years of close association with Wright, I never saw him in a more exuberant mood. So much had contributed to this mood: the success of the five-member subcommittee that had produced the working text for the theological commission meeting (Wright was a member of the subcommittee, and Council reporter Michael Novak was to note that Wright's work had been spectacular); the rousing reception accorded him by his brother-bishops at the Hierarchy meeting (there was a standing ovation for Wright and Auxiliary Bishop James H. Griffiths of New York, another member of the theological commission); and finally the enormous satisfaction of having successfully defended Murray in the very midst of his enemies. It was Wright's great moment at the Council, and Murray's great challenge. Murray did not fail it. The vote to clear the text for general Council debate was taken the next day. It was eighteen to five to release the text—"a glorious victory for the Good Guys," in Murray's words. One of the five negatives belonged to Ottaviani, no doubt.

The big battle had been won, but not yet the war. The fight moved now to the Council floor, and it would be two years, countless strategy sessions, over six hundred written interventions, another one hundred and twenty speeches (many of them written by Murray), and five corrected versions of the text before the vote would finally be taken to close debate on the religious freedom issue. The vote came September 21, 1965, and the Murray-inspired text carried 1,997 to 224; there was one vote spoiled. The text now went to the Secretariat for Christian Unity for final wording and polishing, a perfunctory procedure since under the rules of the Council the text could no longer be essentially changed. Ironically, the person most responsible for the document would not be involved in drawing up this sixth and last text. Murray suffered a lung collapse on October 5, and was rushed to the hospital.

But he was not forgotten, nor would his efforts go unrecognized. A few weeks before the historical approval and promulgation of the religious liberty text, Pope Paul would ask Murray to concelebrate Mass with him in St. Peter's. The Mass was offered on

November 18, and for those looking for symbolism, the occasion was replete with it. There was the one-time pariah now at the altar with the Pope of the Church Universal; there was Murray's long-time nemesis, Cardinal Ottaviani, off in the congregation or somewhere beyond; and there was the Pope announcing at the Mass that the Roman Curia would be reformed and that the procedure would begin with Ottaviani's Congregation of the Holy Office. It was total victory, a magnificent day for the weak and recuperating Murray. He would tell a friend it was one of the most wonderful Masses he had ever celebrated. It had to be the greatest day of his life.

For John Courtney Murray, the importance of the Declaration on Religious Freedom rested on its three doctrinal tenets: "The ethical doctrine of religious freedom as a human right (personal and collective); a political doctrine with regard to the functions and limits of government in matters religious; and the theological doctrine of the freedom of the Church as the fundamental principle in what concerns the relations between the Church and the socio-political order." As mentioned earlier, Murray did not regard the Declaration as a milestone in human history. "In all honesty," he wrote in introducing the Declaration's text in a Council omnibus*, "it must be admitted that

* *The Documents of Vatican II, With Notes and Comments by Catholic, Protestant and Orthodox Authorities;* Walter M. Abbott, S.J., general editor; Joseph Gallagher, translation editor; Guild Press, American Press, Association Press, New York, 1966.

the Church is late in acknowledging the validity of the principle."

Yet the Declaration did catch the Church up with the world, and Murray's insightful mind told him where the next challenge would be. "Inevitably, a second great argument will be set afoot—now on the theological meaning of Christian freedom." For, as he said, those who receive this freedom "assert it within the Church as well as within the world." Indeed, this was to be the great testing of the post-conciliar Church.

Alas, John Courtney Murray was not around to help resolve the issues bound up with these assertions, and those thrusts which he outlined so precisely: "the dignity of the Christian, the foundations of Christian freedom, its object or content, its limits and their criterion, the measure of its responsible use, its relation to the legitimate reaches of authority and to the saving counsels of prudence, the perils that lurk in it, and the forms of corruption to which it is prone." John Courtney Murray would be dead within two years.

In January, 1966, Murray was named to head the newly organized LaFarge Institute at 106 West 56th Street in New York City, a Jesuit think-tank which was to be host to scholars of all persuasions meeting to discuss interreligious and interracial topics. Murray had a sister in Queens, Mrs. Kenneth Williams—Kay —and of a summer's day in 1967 John went out to Kay's home for lunch. He never made it back. John Courtney Murray was stricken with a heart attack in a taxi returning home. The cabbie rushed his fare to

Whitestone General Hospital. Murray, 63, was pronounced dead there. The date was August 16, 1967.

The *New York Times* extended him a celebrity's *vale*: a two-column head, long obituary, a second-day story of tributes, then lengthy funeral coverage. Tributes flowed in from the White House to Rome, from Lyndon Johnson characterizing Murray as one whose life "transcended the barriers of nation, race and creed," from Archbishop Giovanni Benelli conveying Pope Paul VI's admiration for one "who never stinted in the service of God, Church, and the Society of Jesus." The funeral Mass was at St. Ignatius Loyola Church on Park Avenue at 84th Street, the same church where Father Teilhard de Chardin had had his lonesome funeral a dozen years before. The scene was in marked contrast. For Murray, two cardinals were in the sanctuary, Spellman and Cushing. The congregation included more than one hundred bishops and priests, and one thousand friends and admirers. The celebrant was not Murray's Jesuit superior nor a Jesuit colleague. John Courtney Murray was now the soul of institutional respectability. The Mass was celebrated by the Auxiliary Bishop of New York who would be the archdiocese's next Ordinary and its next Cardinal, Terence Cooke.

If the dead can savor irony, Murray must have chuckled all the way to Woodstock—the Maryland one—where he was buried.

In final analysis, John Courtney Murray must be categorized as a two-issue man. He addressed himself to numerous issues of the day, but with nowhere near the depth that he did Church and State, and religious freedom. Nor always with the same degree of perceptiveness. Generally he was on the mark. On birth control, for instance, he was convinced that "the Church reached for too much certainty, too soon, and went too far." Similarly he was aware that the extravagant impulses of the American Church to build—churches, schools, hospitals—and to establish services and organizations that only duplicated those of the civic sector generated an "exclusiveness" that could ultimately be hurtful to the Church as institution. On the other hand, the Joe McCarthy issue passed him by; "Murray was himself not publicly involved," Pelotte was to comment in his book. Further, his position on racial justice, again in Pelotte's words, at one stage reflected "some of the more limited attitudes" of the time. This would be especially true of Murray's 1945 period, when in a memorandum to a superior he could deplore the handling of a racial controversy at St. Louis University, but at the same time say that he was "quite at a loss to detect any grounds for 'sin' in the exclusion of Negroes" from a student prom there, the dance being the bone of contention.

To suggest, as the foregoing does, that John Courtney Murray had limitations of concern is not, however, to discount his meaning nor his accomplishments in his special areas of Church and State and of religious freedom. Murray's basic legacy, as Burghardt was to emphasize at the 1967 meeting of the now defunct Catholic Association for International Peace, was to insert the Catholic Church into history: "he more than any other single individual helped move Catholicism away from classicism into historical consciousness," said Burghardt. No seemingly blind spots in his constitution can diminish that enormous accomplishment.

The paradox is that great as John Courtney Murray was, time is moving him deeper into the shadows of memory and of interest. Before his years ran out, prestigious institutions such as Harvard, Yale, Notre Dame, Georgetown and fifteen more would cue up to bestow honorary degrees on him. Other awards were his for the mere acceptance, as the Christian Wisdom Award from Loyola University of Chicago and the Cardinal Spellman Award of the Catholic Theological Society. Upon his death, Fordham University would name a hall after him and his Jesuit contemporary, Gustave Weigel. But a new generation hardly knows John Courtney Murray. Emmet John Hughes, the same of *Time-Life* and the Eisenhower White House, put aside a planned biography of Murray in favor of a study of the American Presidency; he won't return to the Murray project. And when Pelotte went back to Paulist Press, the publisher of his Murray monograph, with a collection of published and unpublished material of Murray—the unpublished material including many suppressed Murray articles—the manuscript was turned down because the interest was no longer there. At least one other publisher (reportedly Seabury) also declined the manuscript.

One editor who read the manuscript put it bluntly: the ideas are "passé."

It seems a cruel assessment at first hearing, but I don't think John Courtney Murray would quibble with the judgment. He was realist enough to know what his task was and, this being accomplished, where it situated the Church in society. He knew, for instance, that the Church had to rid itself of several centuries of mindset on Church and State and on religious freedom just in order to catch up with the world. His job, as he saw it, was to help with the ridding, and this he did. At the same time he also knew that the world was not going to stand still once the Church had caught up with it, and, concomitantly, that a new set of challenges would be confronting the Church born of the meeting of old ones. He was prepared to grapple with these. Thus, if his ideas now seem "passé" to some, it is only because John Courtney Murray was short-changed on time, the years running out on him after one job was done and before the next one could be suitably addressed. It's happened to other giants of history. It will happen again. John Courtney Murray shouldn't be diminished on such an account as that.

VI

DOROTHY DAY

The Best of Good Samaritans

IN MY SECRET PSYCHE, Dorothy Day has always
had me on the defensive. It isn't that she has been
unpleasant or uncooperative those times when our
paths crossed. Quite the opposite. She has been agree-
able, forth-right—you'd like to say sweetness itself,
except that Dorothy rebels at being called sweet. She
puts me on the defensive by making me aware—by her
mere voice, if we are talking by phone; by her mere
presence, if we happen to be in the one place at the
same time—how much she is that I could never be. By
"she," I mean the Catholic Worker movement as
much as Dorothy herself. It isn't that I aspire to her
intelligence, her large attainments, her honored place
in the religious and secular worlds. Much, much less is
it because I envy her anything about the Catholic
Worker movement. I am on the defensive because I
could never live her life or the life of a Catholic
Worker. I carry a secret shame for that realization.

Throughout my life, many of my closest friends and
working colleagues have been Catholic Worker
"alumni." So are many of those I admire most as
Catholic thinkers and doers. But so far as making the
same *rite de passage* as, say, Jim O'Gara or John
Cogley or Mike Harrington or Tom Cornell or Jim
Forest or Betty Barteleme or Bill Callahan—well, I

just couldn't do it. I'm too much a product—or is the word "victim"?—of the spic'n' span culture. I keep a messy desk, have some messy habits, but I like comfortable beds, clean sheets, well-prepared food, tablecloths, deodorized associates. The Catholic Worker isn't a hygenically contaminated place, and I apologize if I seem to suggest it is; it is rather that in pursuing and exemplifying, quite literally, the corporal works of mercy, the Worker fails my sanitation fetishisms. The problem is with me, not the Worker. I could no more hang around a Catholic Worker house than I could, say, rob a bank or mug an old woman. When I mentioned this once to a Worker alumnus, he said, "Don't think you're so different from Dorothy, or anyone else in the movement for that matter. You could. In a community of love, you rise above tastes and preferences. Actually, it's the least of challenges given the need and the suffering of those the Worker serves." Maybe he is right about motivational effects, although I doubt it in my case, untested as it remains. I just know that my friend's kindly reassurance made me feel more ashamed of myself than before. My brooding continued.

Recently Abigail McCarthy provided some oblique solace, when she allowed in her *Commonweal* column that she "could not completely accept the Worker ideas and the Worker way of living." For my part, I never had particular trouble with the movement's ideas. It was the life style, as I've made humiliatingly clear, that put me off. So I seized on Abigail's "way of living" phrase for some convenient self-justification.

156

Now I wasn't the only one, was I, who felt this way? But the essential point is this—and it was Abigail McCarthy's as well: you don't have to go the O'Gara-Cogley-Harrington, etc., route to be an admirer of Dorothy Day, a fellow-traveler of hers and a partisan of the Catholic Worker movement, just as you don't have to be a Catholic Worker volunteer to benefit spiritually from the what and wherefore of all that she and the movement stand for. Some months ago, Tom Cornell wrote in a Catholic Peace Fellowship appeal letter of how wonderful he found it was to be back at Fellowship headquarters at 339 Lafayette Street in lower Manhattan. (He had been most recently with the Fellowship of Reconciliation at Nyack in suburban Rockland County.) "The Catholic Worker houses are three and four blocks away," he commented. "Needless to say, it is good to keep physically as well as spiritually close to the Worker." He's right, of course. But what Abigail was saying (I think), and what I am convinced of, is that a spiritual affinity with Dorothy Day and the Catholic Worker is possible quite apart from direct personal contact with her or involvement in the movement. It was for me in my Worcester and Pittsburgh years, when Dorothy Day was only a magazine or newspaper picture, fully as much as it has been for me in my New York years, when I could be on the phone occasionally to Dorothy on one matter or another, shaking her hand or just viewing her from apart at some function or event, as a Pax Christi meeting at Manhattan College, or Maisie Ward's funeral, or John Cogley's memorial Mass.

This is a majestically inspirational woman, this Dorothy Day. Notre Dame's Father Theodore M. Hesburgh remarked in 1972, when Dorothy agreed at last to accept a tangible honor from a major American institution—the university's esteemed Laetare Medal—that she "has been comforting the afflicted and afflicting the comfortable virtually all of her life." He didn't need the adverbial qualifier "virtually." Even when life was at loose ends for Dorothy, even when she was a searcher and a groper, adventuring with Communism and rubbing elbows with the great and near-great—Malcolm Cowley, John Dos Passos, Emma Goldman, Mike Gold, John Reed, Max Bodenheim, Eugene O'Neill (the latter harranguing her with Francis Thompson's *The Hound of Heaven*) —even then Dorothy Day was afflicting the comfortable. She was barely 21 when she went to jail for the first time (for demonstrating too strenuously in Washington on behalf of women's voting rights) and almost 80 when she went for what is presumably the last time. Will anyone ever forget that marvelous picture of California marshals, armed with revolvers and billy clubs, arresting the gentle Dorothy for taking part in a protest demonstration in behalf of Cesar Chavez and the United Farm Workers? Or that equally memorable picture of Dorothy with Betty Bartelme, the editor, and Ned O'Gorman, the poet, standing rigidly in Times Square, refusing to go underground as the military played its nuclear cold-war games on the American citizenry and the world? The particular game of the moment was an air-raid drill.

Obviously, Dorothy Day's objectives have been in helping not just those souls bent by hunger and misfortune—although this has been the primary work of the Catholic Worker movement—but also in bearing witness on the large human issues that dramatically affect social climates. Some of these issues have been less conspicuous than war and peace, or even the rights of a minority farm-workers group to organize a union of its own. Some have been virtually forlorn, almost totally obscure, as the issue of the treatment of women in prisons. One of the first members of the "prison faculty" organized by the Institute of Women Today, a new feminist organization concerned about women prisoners, was Dorothy Day. Indeed, who more appropriately than she could have responded to the query of an elderly woman "resident" in a West Virginia women's prison? "Why are you here?" asked the woman. "We have come to wash your feet," answered Dorothy Day.

There are several keys to Dorothy Day in that response: her easy way with people, her humbleness of character and her Christological approach, even to phraseology, to human problems. Hers is a religious commitment and a radicalism brilliantly capsulized by Colman McCarthy in the February 24, 1973 *New Republic*: she has "the wild extreme notion that Christianity is a workable system, the bizarre idea that religion has more to do with what you work at than what you believe." No truer words. Dorothy Day doesn't vote, she doesn't pay taxes, she submits no financial accounting to the Internal Revenue Service of the voluntary contributions that flow in to keep her and the movement going from day to day, seven days a week, fifty-two weeks a year. And for all this she is held in a respect that is unique in America. Several years ago, when the Internal Revenue Service sought to force Dorothy Day and the Catholic Worker to get up $296,359 to satisfy a governmental tax claim extending back over several years, the outcry from the public was such that IRS officials hastily folded their case and retreated in embarrassment to the bureau headquarters. Even the *New York Times* and the *New York Post* had reacted editorially in horror. The brass of the IRS! It was as if American motherhood had been attacked. On settlement day, Dorothy and her colleagues went to the Automat for a lunch of celebration. Later she would say to me, in understatement that belied her stature and that of the Catholic Worker, "They were willing to recognize our undoubtedly religious convictions in our conflict with the state."

The 1972 contention with the Internal Revenue Service dramatizes a curious paradox in Dorothy Day and her regard for authority. Where civil authority is concerned she has ever been the minimalist. She has argued, for instance that "the whole people composing a community should take care of what governing is to be done," rather than the centralized state or national government. Thus would she refuse to vote, to pay taxes, to heed those sirens signaling air-raid practice drills, while she placed her emphases on developing communities of love. It is the formula for the anarchistic society, and indeed in her autobiography *The Long Loneliness** Dorothy Day does say, "I do believe, whether it can be realized or not, that the anarachist society approaches nearer to this ideal of mutual aid than do other forms of government." On the other hand, where ecclesiastical authority is concerned, she is close to being a maximalist. It is well known, for instance, that she refused to let the Worker become a way-station of the underground church, much as Emmaus House, a radical Catholic community in East Harlem, had become. Swinging liturgists have never been her thing. One of her anguished complaints in a 1970 conversation with Dwight Macdonald was of a Dan Berrigan Mass at the New York Catholic Worker. Berrigan, sensitive to Dorothy's feelings, conducted what he thought was a rather orthodox liturgy, but it was not orthodox enough for Dorothy. "He used a loaf of bread for the Host," Dorothy complained to Macdonald, "tore off hunks with his hands, crumbs

* Recently reissued by Curtis Books, along with two other Dorothy Day books: *Loaves and Fishes,* a history of the Catholic Worker movement, and *On Pilgrimage: The Sixties,* a new collection from Dorothy's diary/journal that runs regularly in *The Catholic Worker. From Union Square to Rome,* the book in which Dorothy Day relates the story of her pilgrimage from Communism to Catholicism, was included in the fifty-nine volume set on "The American Catholic Tradition," issued in 1978 by Arno Press.

all over the floor. And later they were swept up and dumped into the garbage pail. If you really believe they had become the flesh of Jesus, as I do, literally— well, that was no way to treat the body of Our Lord. Those crumbs bothered me." This religious reverence is no latter-day preoccupation of hers; further, it extends beyond the Christ of the sacrament to the *alter Christus* of the institution. Dorothy would wince at some of the material appearing in the Chicago *Catholic Worker* edited by Cogley and O'Gara in the years before World War II, fearful that it would be regarded as bishop-baiting. And even in 1952, when she and the Catholic Worker movement were among the few free spirits in the Church, she would still say that "if the Chancery ordered me to stop publishing the *Catholic Worker* tomorrow, I would."

There's a dichotomy, which Dorothy Day herself could never satisfactorily explain, in her approaches to civil and ecclesiastical authority. Part of it stems from her admittedly inconsistent self. "Really, Dwight," she once exclaimed to Macdonald, "you've known me long enough not to expect me to be consistent." But part of it—the ecclesiastical part, that is—is rooted in the intensity of faith and the literalness of her belief in the Church to which she was converted when she was 30. Like the rest of us, she has her occasional bitter moment, but she makes her distinction between "Holy Mother the Church" and "the human element in it." The human element is blameable for such short-comings as she encounters.

Many expect Dorothy Day to be a Church liberal, perhaps because of her radical social and political side, perhaps also because within the Church she has been shrewd enough to exercise the freedoms possible and survive, even in such an authoritative bastion as the Archdiocese of New York. But beware expectations. Dorothy Day willingly subscribes to the reforms of Vatican Council II—indeed subscribes most warmly, for to her many of the old rules were unfair and onerous. She is even willing to press for further legitimate changes. But then she gets cautious. She believes too much in Catholicism, the Pope and the authority of the Church to want to see the Church become what any individual wants it to be for him or her. Anarchy may have more than one meaning, but in her case it does not have two applications. Dorothy Day reads no one out of the Church—"There's room in the Church for everyone," she said in a 1972 *New York Post* interview—but she refuses to look benignly on much that is done in the name of freedom and the liberated conscience. Accordingly, she supports Paul VI on birth control; she deplores do-it-yourself liturgies; and as a person who rises each morning at 6 to pray and who reads the Bible for two hours each day, she regrets seeing religious give up communal prayers . . . to say nothing of nuns' shedding their habits. "I guess I'm pretty much of a conservative in Church matters," she says.

She is. But religious conservatism and secular radicalism blend well in Dorothy Day—to a degree, in fact, that some like *Time* magazine have declared her a saint, to her embarrassment . . . and annoyance. Not surprising. As John Cogley once wrote, Dorothy Day knows "saints" can easily be dismissed as people who are to be admired rather than imitated, and all her life she has been an advocate, a partisan, a social agitator. Yet the unofficial canonization does have a rationale; Dorothy Day does belong to a social and spiritual elite.

By the same token, the Catholic Worker movement fully merits its respected place in American social history: for the charity it has dispensed over the years to tens of thousands through soup kitchens, clothing depots, and via the rooms and bunks of houses of hospitality; as well as for the emphases it has brought—albeit it sometimes chaotically—to questions of poverty, peace, employment, property, pacifism, and justice generally, through Friday night colloquies, *The Catholic Worker*, and the witnessing of movement personnel. It's too bad, come to think of it, that movements cannot be canonized.

It is a fascinating route that Dorothy Day has traveled over her eight decades. She was born in the Bath Beach section of Brooklyn in 1897, the daughter of a vaguely Protestant family. The father's side was Calvinist; the mother's, Episcopal. But belief was regarded within the household as a decidely private matter; "to talk about religion was like baring your soul," Dorothy was to recall. Mr. Day was a newspaperman—sportswriter, actually—and his trade took the family to California, when Dorothy was 6, and to Chicago, when she was 8. (The San Francisco earthquake of 1906 drove the Days back to the mid-West.) Dorothy Day did her growing up in Chicago, a somewhat different person from the Dorothy Day who would one day wear cast-off clothing and blossom under a life of voluntary poverty. In Chicago, she was for a time ashamed of the family's limited means, and she would seek to delude schoolmates into thinking that she lived other than where she did. Of course this was when she was very, very young. Residency was better after three moves. The Days settled on Webster Avenue near Lincoln Park, and Dorothy no longer felt the compulsion to be ashamed of the family's residential circumstances. She would come to feel less than proud of those youthful attitudes of hers, however.

Upton Sinclair s *The Jungle* routed all superciliousness. Dorothy read the book, and soon she was exploring the slums of Chicago's West Side, digging into Peter Kropotkin, the Russian anarchist, and molding the new ideological and religious person. By the time she entered the University of Illinois at Urbana, Dorothy was well on the road to social radicalism—and, though who would have suspected it?, Roman Catholicism. The latter slipped into consciousness in some measure through her admiration of the culture and cohesiveness of Chicago's West Side ethnic neighborhoods. The neighborhoods were heavily Catholic and provided Dorothy with her first direct impressions of Catholic life. The experience influenced her in the direction of the Catholic Church, she would one day admit.

Dorothy Day withdrew from the University of Illinois after two years' study and followed the family to New York, where her father had joined the *Morning Telegraph* as racing editor. She did not enroll in another university. As William D. Miller was to write in *A Harsh and Dreadful Love* (Liveright, 1973), "the formalisms of academic life seemed to suggest not paths but byroads toward that as-yet-unnamed objective to which she felt her life should be directed." Dorothy embarked, instead, on journalism, holding down jobs with the *New York Call*, *The Masses* and *The Liberator*, all left-wing journals, while getting caught up in radical causes, such as the suffragist movement and trade unionism, through the Industrial Workers of the World, the Wobblies. Still groping for life's objective, Dorothy tried nurse's training, slipped off to Europe for six months, returned to Chicago, then located briefly in New Orleans for a stint with the *New Orleans Item*; she wrote a play and a novel, *The Eleventh Virgin*, which was good enough to be picked up by Hollywood for a movie, for the very grand sum in 1924 of $5,000. With the $5,000 she purchased a cottage on Staten Island, and some months later she entered into a common-law relationship with Forster Battingham, a World War I veteran who eventually was to slip into thin air. First would come Tamar, however, the daughter who was to bring so much joy and so many grandchildren (nine) into her life.

It was Tamar who was to trigger the critical decisions in Dorothy Day's life. Battingham was less than enthusiastic about the baby's arrival; as an anarchist, he saw little sense in bringing another child into a world of exploitation and injustice. Tamar was born, nevertheless, and Dorothy, who had begun to reach out seriously to Catholicism in her quest for meaning and purpose, had her baptized. This done, Dorothy felt a compulsion for baptism herself, aware at the same time that baptism would mean separation from Battingham. She went ahead anyway, receiving the sacrament in a church in Tottenville on Staten Island. Battingham went off, and Dorothy, now and forevermore on her own devices, went to Hollywood, which had approached her as a script writer on the basis of her play. Of course she had Tamar with her.

Hollywood was not for Dorothy Day. There was neither work satisfaction nor answer to the questions troubling body and soul. Life was still without large purpose. After three months she picked up her last paycheck, packed up Tamar, and bought a bus ticket for Mexico City. Maybe there. In Mexico, mother and daughter lived among the poor, an ennobling experience for Dorothy, and one which she wrote about for *Commonweal*. But the stay was abbreviated. Tamar developed a digestive disorder, and her ailment forced Dorothy to return to New York. It was May, 1930. Dorothy Day was pushing towards her mid-30s and for her life was aimless yet. She moved into an apartment on Fifteenth Street, took a library-research job, added *America* to her writing outlets—and answered the door one evening in early 1933 to find Peter Maurin at the other end of the knock. She did not sense it at the moment, but meeting Peter Maurin was to resolve all problems of purpose in the life of Dorothy Day.

Peter Maurin was a special kind of man: unwashed, humble but unabashed, Franciscan but unintimidated, uncompromising. A native Frenchman, he lived almost as a Depression hobo, wandering about, bombarding anyone within earshot—on street corner, in drawing room, bus or university cafeteria—with his impassioned social theories. "Peter Maurin always held before our eyes a vision of the new man," Dorothy would recall, "the new social order as being possible, by God's grace, here and now." His approach to social challenges was essentially religious and personalist, his big concern being in helping humankind adjust to the emotional and economic pressures of capitalism and the industrial society. And save their souls at the same time. He believed in a withdrawal from the capitalist system so far as each individual was able to do so.

Peter Maurin had never met Dorothy Day before that evening in 1933. He had read something she had written, and tracked her down through George Shuster of *Commonweal*. For four months he came around daily, and talked to and at her from mid-afternoon until 10 or 11 at night. Dorothy frequently wearied under Peter's lectures, and would try to veer him off onto others. But Peter Maurin kept coming back to Dorothy Day. He brought her books: Church histories, lives of the saints. He brought social commentaries, and these he passed on with ideas of his own. He "converted" her by zeal, persistence and idealism. Dorothy agreed to become editor of the paper Peter had in mind. The paper, of course, was *The Catholic Worker*, the first issue of which rolled from the presses in time for May Day observances, 1933. A gigantic rally was planned in New York City's Union Square, and Dorothy and three circulation recruits headed for it, bravely armed with their four-page tabloid. The results were not spectacular. Two of the recruits were quickly hooted home by the leftist mob, which seized on the word "Catholic" in the paper's title for some irreverent taunting. Dorothy and Joe Bennett hung tough, but they did not sell the issue out, though the crowd numbered 50,000 and the paper was but a penny a copy. The remainder was given away, many being mailed to diocesan newspaper editors, friends and prominent Catholics. The mailed copies produced an encouraging response and some contributions. But if Dorothy Day was encouraged, Peter Maurin wasn't. "Everybody's paper is nobody's paper," he flung at Dorothy after viewing the issue-one layouts. She knew what agitated him. Maurin expected only his essays to appear in the paper, while Dorothy Day, a natural and penetrating writer, had ideas of her own to express. Conceit and vanity on Maurin's part? It would seem so "to the unknowing," Dorothy would say with characteristic charity, but really he was concerned primarily with his "clarification."

Peter Maurin got over his pique with the help of

issue two, an issue which was essentially his. Dorothy Day's editorship was affirmed—"I would rather definitely sign my own work," Maurin wrote—but Peter's ideas were laid out: for houses of hospitality, for "agronomic universities" (read farm communities), for roundtable clarification discussions, for a kind of Utopian Catholic-Christian communism which allowed for private property. "I am not opposed to private property with responsibility," he explained. "But those who own private property should never forget it is a trust." Issue two of *The Catholic Worker* did more than placate Peter Maurin. In effect it established The Catholic Worker as a movement, at the same time that it was cementing the bond between the editor and the visionary.

It has been a matter of speculation since which of the two—Peter Maurin or Dorothy Day—was the principal force in the development of the Catholic Worker into the most vibrant independent social organization of twentieth-century American Catholicism. Dorothy has given all credit to Peter and described herself merely as "the housekeeper" of the movement. But there are those who maintain that it was not Peter but Dorothy and her gentle, effective ways which were essentially responsible for the success of the Worker. John Cogley, who would know as well as anyone, says so. In his memoir, *A Canterbury Tale* (Seabury, 1976), he wrote that "We had no doubt that she was the real leader of the Catholic Worker movement." Peter Maurin, said Cogley, "was obviously uncomfortable in the feigned role of leadership.

Unless the questions were abstractly philosophical or sweepingly historical, he would turn helplessly to Dorothy Day for an answer."

In the long reach of history, it really isn't important which of the two was the "true" leader of the Catholic Worker movement, whether it was Peter Maurin or Dorothy Day. In the context of certain new sensitivities, however, the question is worth touching on, for implicit in the contention that the true leader was Dorothy is the suggestion of a contriving creature, working through a man to exercise a role that society until recently has generally denied to a woman. History is replete with instances of women achieving their goals through men, but that the Peter Maurin-Dorothy Day association is another such an instance is debatable. Dorothy Day bristles at the idea, and rightly so. So do admirers such as Abigail McCarthy. "She is very sure of which half of the world's population she belongs to," Abigail remarks in rejecting the manipulative notion. Mrs. McCarthy views the association of the two as a harmonic reaffirmation of the vital need of one sex for the other in common endeavors.

On the other hand, if it is true, as Dorothy would have it, that Peter Maurin deserves "all credit"— Cogley's phrase—for the Worker movement, it is no less true that "all credit" is Dorothy's for the last three decades and more. Peter Maurin died May 15, 1949. The original vision was his, but the latter-day direction, going back well before 1949 when Peter was aging and infirm, has entirely been hers. Not surprisingly, the Catholic Worker movement is synonymous with the name Dorothy Day, *not* Peter Maurin.

Spectacular as is the record of the Catholic Worker movement, it has not always been measurable. The movement has never been strong on detail, nor self-righteous and proud to the point of keeping running tallies on the numbers of people clothed, of hungry fed, of tired bedded for the night. The Catholic Worker movement just isn't the United Way. The charity it practices is anonymous and unrecorded, pure and unselfish in the fullest of senses. Perhaps the only thing in the movement known for sure is the circulation of *The Catholic Worker,* and that's only because printers and Postal Service officials keep count in order to be paid for services rendered. It's 90,000 copies, at a penny a copy, nine times a year. (The annual subscription price is 25 cents, which makes the *Worker* almost three times more expensive to subscribe to by the year than to buy copies individually—a small anomaly but only one at the Worker.)

No one, in fact, is ever quite sure from one day to the next how many houses of hospitality there are. Houses of hospitality spring up sometimes without Dorothy's knowing beforehand about them. Once "discovered," however, Dorothy watches over them, making it a point to visit each house, new or old, as regularly as possible. An inveterate traveler, she seems always to be "On Pilgrimage" to houses of hospitality, and her column in *The Catholic Worker* is taken up largely by an account of these travels. Houses of hospitality can be as near as Pittsburgh and South Bend or as far away as Australia, where there is a Catholic Worker farming commune of families as well. She's visited there, too.

But just as houses of hospitality can spring up unannounced, so can they fade away as quietly. And do. The movement attracts young people by and large, and young people tend to go off one day to get married, to settle down and pursue careers of their own. At the same time, the needs of a community might change, phasing out one kind of witness in favor of another.

At one time there were as many as forty Catholic Worker communities in the United States alone: farming communes, urban houses of hospitality, even artisan communities. There are fewer now, but some really unique ones, as the houses of hospitality that exist to assist families of inmates at the federal reformatory for women in Alderson, West Virginia, and at Folsom Prison in California. A particularly impressive Worker house, and one that recently underwent a traditional Catholic Worker trauma, is the one in Los Angeles. It runs a house of hospitality, medical clinic, and serves up to a thousand meals a day in an old two-story hotel in the city's skid-row sector. The word on the street was that the Worker had the "best food on the row" and some of the best services. But suddenly the house's existence was in jeopardy. Ownership of the building changed hands, and the rent shot from $475 to $1700 a month. At the same time all maintenance was suspended. The Los

Angeles Catholic Worker community first tried to negotiate; no success. Then it hunted for other accommodations in square-mile skid row. Finally the owner, faced with possible loss of tenant, sat down with community representatives and accepted $9,000 —the last cent in the community's savings account— towards purchase of the property. Needed now, in about six weeks' time, was $55,000, else the community would be out both its $9,000 and its occupancy.

"On the face of it, the situation seemed impossible," said Catherine Morris of the Los Angeles community. "We don't have a lot of wealthy or powerful friends to turn to; our friends are the people we live with and serve. But we were trusting that people who see our need and the urgency of the situation would be moved to stand with us."

Well, miracles always seem to happen where the Catholic Worker is concerned. An appeal went out, and within two weeks the Los Angeles community had its $55,000, much of it through small contributions. It was the good news story of Summer, 1977; but, again, a typical Catholic Worker story.

The Catholic Worker may be spread quite literally over country and world, but wherever its communities are, the heart and soul of the movement remain in New York: in the house of hospitality at 36 East First Street, successor to earlier houses on Mott Street, Chrystie Street and elsewhere. In the converted school building nearby, which is haven for homeless "shopping bag ladies." And in "the farm with a view" at

Tivoli, one hundred miles north of New York City, on the upper Hudson, where most of the New York community's activities shift to when the summer sun oppresses the Bowery.

Heart and soul of the Catholic Worker movement are in New York, because New York is where Dorothy Day is. Indeed, so much is she the heartbeat of the movement, the ensoulment of its principles, that one worries what will happen to it once Dorthy, in her 80's and in frail health as this was written, is no longer around. People of the movement are concerned, but they are not in panic. "We have Dorothy now," Catholic Worker Peggy Scherer said recently to *Newsweek* magazine, "but we will always have the Gospel." It is a brave enough comment, but nothing on which to stake the future of the movement, particularly one without strong central organization and one so heavily dependent on charism. Once there were two charismatic figures at the Worker, and after Peter was gone there was Dorothy. Is there another Peter, another Dorothy standing in the wings? It would be extraordinarily good luck if there were, and an extraordinary distribution of charism in a single movement. But then, as I've said, the Worker has known its miracles.

Yet perhaps one should not worry too much about the Catholic Worker's future, for it has always been able to attract outstanding talent, even non-Catholic talent. Most recent issues of *The Catholic Worker,* for instance, list as managing editor Robert Ellsberg, son of Daniel Ellsberg, the Vietnam-era anti-war activist. Ellsberg is not a Catholic. The problem is that despite many gifted and dedicated Workers, some of them "old-timers" in the movement—people like Stanley Vishnewski and Marty and Rita Corbin—the Worker remains a transient institution. It appeals to the best and the brightest, the most highly motivated, but it does not hold but a handful for more than a relatively brief period of time. Those associated with the movement never lose their love and affection for it, at least none that I regard, and many go back periodically for spiritual refreshment and renewal. There is a fascinating account in the July, 1977, issue of *Mother Jones* of Mike Harrington back for a Friday night colloquy, discussing with shopping bag ladies the nuances of welfare state capitalism, incremental reform and democratic socialism. But the alumni don't stay; they return to the larger world—to which they bring, to be sure, touches of the idealism and inspiration that mark the Catholic Worker movement, a good thing in itself. But the Worker is left pretty much where it was a few hours before.

This is not said in criticism of any individual, but rather to point up a critical limitation of the movement itself: the Catholic Worker is not large enough, nor organized enough to sustain indefinitely the spiritual, physical and intellectual energies of all who would be associated with it. But, then again, why should it? the Catholic Worker was never conceived as a giant welfare agency, a Department of Health, Education and Welfare, which one entered and there found a career. It was conceived rather as a leaven of society, a voluntary association that would witness to the needs of humanity, harangue about the failures of the system, and personify the essential goodness of individuals in responding to the deprivations and wants of the less fortunate. In this context, the Catholic Worker movement does not need long-term, much less lifetime, commitments from any except that relatively small number necessary to keep it functioning from one day to the next. Rather more does it need a continuing influx of volunteer idealists to keep it alive and vibrant. In other words, precisely the type people that the Catholic Worker has been able to attract in the past, and the type people that nourish it at the present.

With people such as these, the Catholic Worker movement will as easily survive Dorothy Day's death, as the movement and Dorothy herself survived the passing of Peter Maurin. It's as sure as tomorrow.

VII

DOCTOR TOM DOOLEY

The Unquiet American

TOM DOOLEY'S NAME hadn't been in my mind for years, then suddenly twice it was returned within days to memory. The first time was upon reading a news story that the San Francisco/New York foundation bearing his name—The Thomas A. Dooley Foundation, Inc.—had been bilked of $300,000 or more by unidentified employees of a California bank. The second time was through an inquiry from my daughter, a flight attendant with a national airlines. She had been invited by a passenger—a Dooley Foundation official, it developed—to volunteer for a medical project in the Far East. "Did you ever hear of Tom Dooley, Dad?"

Hear of Tom Dooley? Good Lord! Back in the 1950s, Tom Dooley was the paragon of all virtue, the knight in shining armor, the ultimate good Samaritan, the epitome of all that was noble about America and right about Catholicism. Who hadn't heard about Tom Dooley, except maybe someone who was too young to remember the 1950s? My daughter was not yet ten when Tom Dooley died at 34 in 1961. On the other hand, she was almost as young when John F. Kennedy was assassinated, yet John Kennedy is a part of her memory—and that of her younger sister and younger brothers, who (wouldn't you guess?) hadn't heard of Tom Dooley either. Now there's a big difference, naturally, between a President of the United States and a humanitarian doctor working in the teeming cities and forests of the Far East. But time was when this future President was a relatively obscure Senator and when this doctor dwarfed him in fame and recognition. The Gallup Poll, for instance, once listed Tom Dooley seventh among the ten most admired persons in the world, in company with Winston Churchill, Dwight D. Eisenhower and Pope John XXIII. Kennedy would make that list only later.

The point is not so much that history has reversed the recognition factors of the two men. That you would expect by nature of the ultimate office achieved by one of the two. Becoming President is no mean thing. We remember Millard Fillmore, but no physician of his time; yet there must be some doctor of the day who is as deserving of remembrance as poor Millard. We remember President Eisenhower, but not his famous doctor, Paul Dudley White. The point is not that Tom Dooley is not as famous as President Kennedy, but that Dooley should be so quickly and completely fled from memory fifteen years after his death.

In the 1950s Tom Dooley seemed destined to endure as a towering American legend, a Clara Barton, Babe Ruth, George Marshall, Abe Lincoln all wrapped up in one. At best he's a very minor legend now. The clouds of the 1960s gathered ominously over a lot of American heroes, and not even Tom Dooley was spared. In 1969 Nicholas von Hoffman wrote in *The Critic:* "Today, after eight years of painful sensitizing to realities unseen in 1961 (the year Tom Dooley died), we might still call him a saint . . . Eight years hence he may be forgotten."

Indeed he was in my household.

Thomas Anthony Dooley III was born in St. Louis on January 17, 1927, into a comfortable middle-class Roman Catholic family. His father was an alumnus of St. Louis University, an officer of the American Car and Foundry Company, a veteran of World War I. His mother was a Wise, of the Pennsylvania Wises, and an Army widow (her first husband was an Air Force pilot who died in a crash in Hickham Field in Hawaii after World War I). She remarried in 1925 and raised a family of four boys, the oldest, Earle, being of her first marriage. Tom, the first of the new marriage, was followed at two-year intervals by Malcolm and Edward. They were a close-knit family, and they came through the Depression with no searing memories of want or need, but fond memories of fun and games, and summers spent at Green Lake, Wisconsin, and Spring Lake, New Jersey. As Malcolm was to recall, "In those quiet summers before World War II, the Dooley boys had their world with vanilla icing on it."

Tom Dooley went to grade school at Barat Hall, zipped through St. Louis University High School in three years (his graduation present was a trip to Mexico), and enrolled as a pre-medical student at Notre Dame University. He was thrilled with himself. Tall, slender, handsome, he could speak French, play the piano, jitterbug like a Hollywood extra. He spoke of one day being a "society doctor" specializing in obstetrics; he was to do a lot of obstetrics work, but as social physician rather than society doctor. It was his choice. Tom Dooley got much more serious about life and the world than those around him in those days ever thought he would.

The sobering began when Earle went away to World War II. Tom announced that he could not "go on at Notre Dame, while Earle is fighting in Europe," and with parental permission he joined the Navy as a medical corpsman. Actually his parents looked on the Navy experience as a convenient test of his vocation to be a doctor. Mr. Dooley never believed that Tom had the patience for the work, and he felt that the stint in the Navy would rout impractical illusions from his head. He was wrong. Tom Dooley worked in a number of Navy and Marine hospitals, and returned to Notre Dame in 1946 more convinced than ever about becoming a doctor. In fact just as soon as he had enough medical-school credits he jumped Notre Dame for St. Louis University School of Medicine, and it was there that he obtained his medical degree. That degree did not come easily. Dooley and St. Louis University didn't mix well. He encountered serious difficulties with members of the medical school faculty, was called before the dean on more occasions than one to explain "unscheduled medical activities," and was even made to repeat his final year. Moreover, St. Louis University School of Medicine refused the required recommendation for Dooley to obtain a Naval commission as a doctor: he had to talk his way back into uniform. The experience long rankled. Years later he would complain bitterly in a letter home from Asia of the "hard and humiliating fight" it was for him to become a doctor.

Not surprisingly, the alma mater of his heart—this, remember, was back in the days when alma maters were forever fondly cherished—was Notre Dame. Tom Dooley never received Notre Dame's undergraduate degree (there would be an honorary degree for him later), but he could be as schmaltzy about the university, the Grotto and the Lady in Blue as a Notre Dame drunk at a party after the USC game. And ever was. "Away from the Grotto, Dooley just prays," he wrote in 1960 to Notre Dame president Father Theodore Hesburgh. "But at the Grotto, especially now when there must be snow everywhere and the lake is ice glass, and that triangular fountain on the left is frozen solid, and all the priests are bundled in their too-large, too long black coats and the students wear snow boots. . . . If I could go to the Grotto now, then I think I could sing inside. I could be full of faith and poetry and loveliness and know more beauty, tenderness and compassion." Notre Dame had the letter engraved, mounted on a plaque and erected at the Grotto.

Tom Dooley completed medical school in 1953, and as Lieutenant Junior Grade Thomas A. Dooley, III, United States Navy, he shipped to a corner of the world that most Americans knew at the time only vaguely, but which they would come to know intimately and painfully. That part of the world was Indochina. Dooley arrived there by way of Camp Pendleton and Japan, and the 1954 Geneva truce between the French and the forces of Ho Chi Minh that provided for a division of the country and a grace period for the resettlement of Vietnamese according to their ideological preferences. Tom Dooley would be assigned to the task group that would assist in the evacuation of those who wished to transfer from the area north of the 17th Parallel, which was to be under Communist control, to the area south of the Parallel, which was to be non-Communist and by easy definition "free." Several months were allowed for the transfer, and millions, quite literally, would move from one zone to the other, the vast majority from the north to the south. The migration southward, by foot and by Navy carrier, would arrest the would's attention and come to be known as the great "Passage to Freedom," a misnomer as it turned out but a marvelously appealing phrase in the cold-war era.

At the center of events was Dr. Tom Dooley, and he was no mere junior medical officer tapping chests, checking coughs and dusting with DDT, at least not for long. An energetic, colorful guy with a keen sense of righteousness and for the dramatic, he was to become symbol and propagandist for a national policy that was garlanded with humanitarianism, but which was laced below the surface with that unique brand of anti-Communist politics that has been the bane of United States diplomacy for a generation and more.

Two things set Tom Dooley up for the role he was to play: his Catholicism and his patriotism. He was a believer, a passionate believer, in the God-and-Country sense that long was the ideal of the pulpit and the schoolroom. Tom Dooley had to be the priest's pet and the general's boast. It never occurred to him for a minute that Christianity—more specifically, Catholicism—and Americanism could not be but coinciding concepts. "Now (the 'Viets') are seeing Americans for themselves, and they find that we are a gentle people." . . . "I am thankful for things that now seem very close at hand, and before were only words— like freedom, liberty, and Catholicism." The thoughts were his during his Haiphong duty. . . . "These villagers have no concept of what has happened in the political field. They have no idea of the rift the world has suffered. They understand nothing about the two camps of ideas of God-loving men and the Godless men." This was Tom Dooley from Laos.

Dooley's were biased, one-dimensional sentiments, as politically primitive, one observer would remark, as the Asian witch doctory and folk medicine that he fought against while treating the sick. In another person the sentiments might have been innocent, but not in one with Tom Dooley's flair for pen and platform. Tom Dooley was soon traveling between ships lecturing crews engaged in the Passage to Freedom operation on the history of Vietnam and the why and wherefore of American involvement in Southeast Asia. He was writing letters home with instructions to get word around on just who the good guys and the bad guys were. Books came next, and the books became bestsellers and influenced millions. The Dooley writing style was populist, perfect *Reader's Digest* material, and indeed, *Reader's Digest* was quickly his unofficial sponsor (remaining so even unto 1976, when it published an article on him entitled "Unforgettable Tom Dooley"). The message infusing all Dooley's writing was God and Country, and in the Lord's Prayer he found the phrase that summed up both his philosophy and his first book, "Deliver us from evil." The evil? Communism, of course. He used the phrase as the title for the book. Over a half-million copies were sold, *Reader's Digest* ran a condensation, and Tom Dooley was now the most celebrated spokesman on the side of a strong American commitment in Southeast Asia. As such he played an instrumental role—perhaps even the instrumental role—in creating the climate of opinion that made escalated involvement and the Vietnam war itself possible.

It is a matter of conjecture how witting a role Tom Dooley played in all of this—whether he was acting on his own, out of purely personal motives, for ends he himself controlled; or whether he was part of some larger script devised by a government that owned his allegiance, shared his ideological biases, and, with or without his knowledge and direct acquiescence, chose to use him. Framing the possibilities in question form, did Tom Dooley pass from Navy doctor to secret American agent? The Chinese and the Viet Cong were convinced he did. Time and again they denounced Tom Dooley as a spy, an advance man for neo-colonialism, a conduit for guns and supplies to anti-revolutionary elements. Dooley resented the accusations and vehemently denied them. But of course he would, say the cynics. Protestations of innocence are the agent's first line of defense, always.

I confess to an ambivalence on the subject. For pro-Dooley purists, it must be reassuring that in the early and mid-1970s, when covers were coming off all sorts of secret American operations, current and historical, there were no revelations involving their hero. It is impossible to believe that, were there secrets to be revealed, they would have stayed secret. On the other hand, so many coincidences in his life make it difficult for anyone to be convinced that there was not a tie-in of some kind between Dooley the doctor and the secret side of his government, that he was not an intelligence agent by some definition of the word. After all he did boast in one of his books about organizing Vietnamese shoeshine boys into a "good intelligence network" to spy on the Communists—although, in defense of Dooley, he was a Navy man then, a part of the team and playing in a game in which intelligence is as legitimate a tactic as an end run in a football contest. The more nagging question is whether he functioned in an agent capacity after he resigned from the Navy and was about his humanitarian missions in Southeast Asia ostensibly as a civilian medical doctor. It is hard to drive away suspicions that the answer is yes. So many wondrous things happened: airplane fuel that materialized out of nowhere when needed to get pharmaceutical supplies into a war zone in northern Laos; the doors that opened, as if by magic, at the highest levels of state wherever Dooley appeared,

Vientiane, Manila, etc.; the special dedication of volunteers who rotated in and out of Dooley's missions. No convergence of stars and planets, no unlimited measure of what Dooley liked to call his "Irish luck" seems able to explain all the "miracles" that happened.

But what quickens suspicion in my mind that very likely Dooley was an agent of some sort is the abrupt suddenness with which he quit the Navy. There is nothing to explain his resignation except maybe an assumption of new official duties undertaken by special request. Certainly the Navy was Dooley's life. He loved it, thrived in it, intended to make it his career. Further, as a man of talent and supreme ambition, he was rocketing towards the top. So certain seemed Dooley's future in the Navy, and the Navy's commitment to Tom Dooley, that the Surgeon General of the Navy was speaking of the day when Dooley would occupy his desk. "It is my earnest hope that good health and good fortune will continue to march with you along tomorrow's road and that some day you may become the Surgeon General of the Navy," Rear Admiral Lamont Pugh wrote Dooley in September, 1954, "not merely because you say that is what you want to be, but because I will leave that office soon with a sense of contentment that it will be in most worthy and 'can do' hands if it ever reaches yours." This was the year before Dooley was ordered back to the United States, presumably for duty at the U.S. Naval Hospital at Bethesda. Those orders were altered, however, and Dooley was attached instead to the office of the Surgeon General. It was to be a three-month assignment and, if you believe his mother's suggestion, it was arranged for Dooley's convenience. *Deliver Us from Evil* was due from the presses, and allegedly it was thought that it would be more convenient for Dooley the author if he was holding down a desk job in Washington rather than orthopedics duty at Bethesda. It was a solicitousness unique in the annals of American military history.

In any case, one evening in February—we're now into the new year of 1956—Tom Dooley returned home from the office and announced to his mother, with whom he was living in Washington, that he was leaving the Navy. The book that he was so anxious about, that the Navy was so interested in (not only had Dooley's special duty been arranged, but the Chief of Naval Operations, Admiral Arleigh Burke had himself written the foreword for the book)—that book was not yet even in the stores.

Throughout his life Tom Dooley shared his soul, his secret thoughts with his mother, but in her generally informative memoir *Promises to Keep,** she is no information source on the resignation. Dooley hits her with the news, direct and blunt: "I'm resigning from the Navy, and I'm going to Laos." The "why" of this sudden, dramatic decision is handled almost in parenthetical phrase: he wants to return to Indochina with a medical team of his own. (Why, one wonders, the

---

* Subtitled "The Life of Doctor Thomas A. Dooley," by Agnes W. Dooley, Farrar, Straus and Co., 1962.

compulsion for a medical team of his own when he was
so content a member of the Navy's medical team, and
so prominent a personality that he could virtually write
his own ticket for the future, or the present?) Mrs.
Dooley's emphasis is on the "how" of it all.

"Before I could recover from the shock," Dooley's
mother writes, "he related how, a few evenings before,
he had gone to dinner in the Vietnam Embassy." She
reports he had a "premonition" that any chance he
had of returning to Indochina with a medical team of
his own hinged on that dinner. Mrs. Dooley continues:
"The Ambassador had invited some Cambodian and
Laotian diplomats to meet Tom. After dinner Tom
talked about the kind of medical mission he had in
mind—small, privately financed by funds which he
would raise by his own efforts, by writing, lecturing,
begging. There would be no political or religious
sponsorship. Neither the government nor the Church
would be involved. The team would consist of himself
and a few young Americans who had served with him
in Vietnam. He said that perhaps, if they did a good
job, they would inspire other Americans, doctors and
laymen, to follow their example of international cooperation on a people-to-people basis."

Well, of course, the idea of the 29-year-old doctor
was snapped up by the sage Asians, and Tom Dooley's
medical mission to the Far East became reality almost
with the speed of light. But the wonder of it all: that a
person with little except enormous self-confidence
could sell so much at that one embassy dinner; that a
man whose life had been so exact a fusion of Catholi-

cism and patriotism would now be so intent on separating himself from religious and governmental sponsorship. The latter wonder increases upon further reflection, for Tom Dooley's Catholicism and his patriotism if anything actually grew in ardor. If there was a priest anywhere within reach, Tom Dooley was at daily Mass. And he waved the flag for all the world like Cardinal Spellman. In Laos, for instance, he flew the American flag from his jeep, and he distributed miniature American flags to his patients, almost as if the flags were medicine for the spirit, which in Dooley's mind they might have been.

Of course it is perfectly possible that in his doctoring and his propagandizing Dooley was acting on his own, and that if he was part of some secret Washington scheme, it was without conscious, formal collusion of his own. But if you believe that, you still have to explain the religion-and-patriotism riddle. The man who would evacuate a five-foot Lady of Fatima statue from Haiphong and bring it triumphantly to Saigon wrapped in an American-Aid blanket does not seem the type who overnight would be insistent on establishing a distance in his life and in his work between the religion and government that that statue and blanket epitomized. The riddle is rendered the more puzzling by the fact that Dooley proposed to make the witness of Catholicism and the ideals of the American system the inspirations and guidelines of his new venture.

Dooley's venture took shape under the name Medico— Medical International Cooperation Organization. It was startlingly idealistic and blessedly naive. "We actually believe that we can win the friendship of people only by working beside them, on equal terms, humans to humans, towards goals that they understand and seek themselves," Dooley declared at the press conference announcing the program. "Medico is a person-to-person, heart-to-heart program. It will aid those who are sick and by that simple act it will win friendship for America." Medico would initiate programs; the host nation would sustain and maintain them after the departure of the Dooley team; the charism would be supplied by Tom Dooley.

His was a fervor common enough in its time, and Dooley would not be the last to identify all good with America and to see American friendship as an unmitigated desirable. He was only the most immediate popular example of the patriotic believer that was. The decade, remember, was the '50s. The age of cynicism was still a few years off. There were yet Galahads abroad in the land.

Giving Dooley his due, agent or not he was among the noblest visionaries that this country or any other ever produced. And if agent he was, that was by far the lesser side of him and his work. He had his faults. His ego rubbed many persons the wrong way. People complained about his "fanatical" zeal, his penchant for personal publicity. They complained even about the medicine he practiced. Speaking of one Asian facility, Dooley admitted that he ran a nineteenth-century hospital. "Upon my departure," he said, "the hospital may drop to the eighteenth century. This is fine, because previously the tribes in the high valleys lived, medically speaking, in the fifteenth century." When all the complaints were toted up, however, Tom Dooley stood head and shoulders above his critics and those smiling, less abrasive American hucksters, the dispensers of guns, butter, Coca-Cola, shaving cream and other artifacts of the so-called good life. The good Tom Dooley did was genuine and addressed to real human needs. In seven years as a doctor in the Far East, he treated hundreds of thousands, quite literally; in less than five years with Medico, he was responsible for the establishment of seven hospitals in five Asian countries. At several of these he was not only the founding physician but the hospital's 24-hour doctor-on-duty. It's hard to fault that record.

As agent or physician, Dooley's mission took him to Nam Tha, a remote village in the northernmost tip of Laos; to Muong Sing, only six miles from the Chinese border; and on "house calls" deep into the jungle. As doctor, he was a general practitioner in the most literal of senses. He treated lepers, men with yaws, children with whooping cough, tubercular women, young pregnant girls, victims of smallpox. He obviously loved people and was especially touched by children. In their welfare he saw the stakes of the big East-West chess game that he wanted to have an effect upon as a major roving piece. "The child here is different from the American child only in geography, chronology, dress and opportunity," Tom Dooley once wrote from Nam Tha. "The American child has the advantages of civilization and the security of being in a free land.

The Lao child (identical in body and soul) has no advantages and little security. His nation is a pawn in a game of power between Slavery and Freedom. There is a simple, clean-cut vivid challenge to those who live in freedom. This challenge demands that to those in need we give some of our time, some of our humanity, some of our life, and some of whatever light we may have to give." Again, ideology cuts across the grain of Dooley's idealism.

Yet this was the stuff Americans could not only listen to believingly in the 1950s, but to which they could be expected to respond affirmatively. Tom Dooley accordingly was on a virtual shuttle back and forth to the United States rallying public opinion behind his work and in behalf of "Freedom's" concerns in the Far East. (Read "American" for "Freedom.") He lectured from one end of the country to the other, gave interviews, wrote articles, went on radio and television. In no time, Tom Dooley Fan Clubs had sprouted up, and pharmaceutical companies were competing with one other to donate medical supplies to Dooley's work. Very quickly Tom Dooley stood enshrined as the true Quiet American—no mere *Quiet* American, no bumbling do-gooder, but the embodiment of an American excellence, a living patriot in doctor's apron. A saint.

A leading hit-parade song at the time was "Hang Down Your Head, Tom Dooley," a ditty about another Tom Dooley who was about to go to the gallows for some foul deed or another. The song distressed Dr. Dooley adorers; Mrs. Dooley even had to have her phone number changed because of all the calls the song brought to her listed number. But good fortune flowed steadily in Tom Dooley's direction in those days, and that mournful song had the curious effect of dramatizing the doctor's name further and increasing donations to Medico. Serendipity. But not everyone was reconciled. Members of a Fort Worth family took the trouble to reword the tune. Their version:

> Lift up your heart, Tom Dooley,
> Your work will never die.
> You taught us to love our neighbor
> And not just to pass him by. . . .

Tragically by then Tom Dooley was ill, fatally so, and the nation whose chest had swelled in admiration for the man was plunged overnight into spasms of sorrow for him. Tom Dooley had cancer. No gallows were his, but he was indeed about to die.

Dooley contracted cancer in 1959. He had been a man of exeedingly good health. In Vietnam, for instance, when Americans were coming down all around him with malaria, dysentery and regional and occupational diseases of multiple sorts, Dooley sailed along as if in some enclosed capsule of protective medicine. "My intestines must be lined with lead," he wrote in the journal he sent his mother from Vietnam. There would be occasional drops in weight, sometimes of an alarming number of pounds, but this generally was from overwork and living on field rations or worse. A short furlough and a few Navy steaks would return him to the 180 pounds at which his six-foot frame best functioned.

The cancer occurred while he was working at Nam Tha. In February, 1959, he and his aides set off on a trip to villages up the Nam Tha River where misery and disease were "rampant," and where, coincidentally (want to be suspicious again?) they had heard radio reports of border infiltrations and skirmishes involving Communists. If theirs was to be other than a medical mission, Dooley provided no clue, except that he seemed to hate going on the trip. He called it a "journey into wretchedness, misery, stink and poverty." But loving the people and agonizing over their lot (I'm now giving him the benefit of all doubt), he went. Unquestionably as doctor he was needed. In one hamlet of one hundred persons, Ban Saly, he found eighty percent of the people ill in one way or another: malaria, tuberculosis, pneumonia, hookworm, anemia and "always" malnutrition. "The people of Laos are not a carefree, happy people," he wrote back. "They laugh and smile, but they suffer." So did Dooley.

On the eleventh day of the trip, the Dooley party arrived at the confluence of the Nam Tha and Mekong Rivers and began poling towards the village of Ban Houei Sai. At nightfall, still short of their destination, the group put ashore in order to make an encampment. As Dooley climbed the embankment, he tripped on the lace of his boot and plunged down a 25-foot drop, gashing his head and badly bruising the right side of his chest wall, just below the shoulder. "I did not of course realize it," Dooley was to say later, "but that fall was to become a pivotal point in my life." Within four months a lump had appeared on his upper chest the size of a golf ball, and the pain in his arm was such that he could not even play the piano that usually relaxed him so. A visiting doctor friend cut the growth away, and took a specimen to Bangkok for analysis. It was diagnosed as a secondary stage of malignant melanoma. A cancerous tumor. Tom Dooley headed back to the United States for deep surgery.

He was a remarkably composed individual. As a doctor, Dooley knew the full extent of his illness, his low chances of survival, but he was determined not to give up his "loving passion for life" because of some shadows on a page." He entered Memorial Hospital on New York City's East 68th Street on August 24, 1959, and along with him came the cameras of CBS. Never one to let a publicity opportunity slip, Tom Dooley elected to have his operation done for television. It would be made into the documentary *Biography of a Cancer.* It was all very gruesome, and typically Dooley. And totally sad. In one of the final scenes of the documentary, Tom Dooley got the word from his surgeon: "Tom, I have some good news for you. The report from the Pathology Department indicates there is absolutely no evidence of this disease anywhere in the tissues that I removed in operation." The doctor was speaking clap-trap. His patient was a very, very sick man. Within a year and a half, Tom Dooley would be dead.

The end was gallant. Tom Dooley finished his third book and criss-crossed the country on a lecture tour that had him delivering forty-nine speeches in thirty-seven cities and raising almost one million dollars for Medico. Then in December—on Christmas Day, actually—he was back in Muong Sing, finding everything just as he left it. "There are twenty-six patients in the ward, and the clinic looks neat and clean—everything shipshape. The boys have done a magnificent job." Tom Dooley was determined to go on, but the end was foreboded by small things. "My next letters will have to be short," he wrote his mother on January 18, 1960, "because it hurts me to type." In a year to the day he would be dead. But what an incredible year: three Asian trips, the opening of a new hospital at Ban Houei Sai, a visit to Rome, an audience with Pope John XXIII, more lectures, publication of another book, more fund-raising, more medicine practiced, two more medical checkups in New York. Finally the body was worn out. Tom Dooley could neither outrun nor outwork death.

Everyone knew death was coming—especially Tom Dooley, who now needed a back brace to support his cancerous vertebrae. His "Iron Maiden" he called it. There were pathetic farewells, in Laos, in Cambodia, in Saigon, in Bangkok. On December 23, 1960, Father John Boucher of Holy Redeemer Church in Bangkok responded to a Tom Dooley phone call to come to the Erawan Hotel. He found Tom lying on a mattress on the floor, the telephone beside him; it hurt too much to use the bed. Tom explained that he wanted to be sure that he received Communion on Christmas Day; Father Boucher gently suggested that he might be thinking more immediately of Extreme Unction. "It might help you," the priest said. Tom agreed.

On Christmas, a spot was arranged for Tom Dooley in the choir loft for Midnight Mass. But he never made it. "Last night was a pretty bad one," he told Father Boucher, when the priest came to Dooley's room on Christmas morning to provide the ministry Tom could not avail himself of at midnight. "As I gave him Communion," the priest recalled, "Tom cried softly." The bravest sometimes do.

Tom Dooley left Bangkok that night for New York on a Pan American plane, refusing helping hands and insisting on making it aboard totally on his own strength, such as was left of it. The space of a double seat was arranged for him better to endure the flight.

Within two days Tom Dooley was back in Memorial Hospital. In three weeks' time he was dead. America wept. Much of the world mourned.

As indicated back in the first paragraph of this chapter, Tom Dooley's work goes on. Not through Medico, however. Nine months after Dooley's death, Medico was superseded by The Thomas A. Dooley Foundation. The explanation was that people close to Dooley, including his mother, felt that Medico had "deviated"—her word—from the objectives Tom Dooley had defined. "I would not have established The Thomas A. Dooley Foundation," she stated in *Promises to Keep*, "if the organization which he had brought into being had really carried on his work." She offers no further detail. In the months before he died, Tom Dooley was said to be disenchanted with certain administrative aspects of Medico. Nevertheless the speed with which Medico was scuttled in favor of a new organization was astonishing. Did the past really have to be shed that fast? Could not the problems be corrected short of the establishment of another organization? Tendentious questions, but unfortunately they have to be asked.*

The Thomas A. Dooley Foundation went on to initiate a number of medical projects in Nepal, Laos, Cambodia, India, Vietnam: clinics, hospitals, mobile health services, laboratory and midwife training courses, teaching programs and the like. Some were short-term projects and completed in due course; some suffered apparent abridgement because of the war and political upheavals in Indochina. A fact sheet sent me by the Foundation in 1977 listed four projects current, all in Nepal; a volunteer program in the fields of

* Mrs. Dooley's assertion that she "established" the Dooley Foundation (p. 249 of *Promises to Keep*) does not coincide by common use of the language with Foundation literature. Accordingl to it, the Foundation "was founded" by Dr. Verne Chaney, in September, 1961. Chaney was a personal friend and surgical consultant to Dooley in Cambodia and Vietnam in 1960, and after Dooley's death left private practice in California to continue and expand the medical programs started by Dooley in Asia.

medical care, social welfare and education; and a scholarship program for training in public health and the health sciences.**

The inspiration for this work remains Dr. Tom Dooley—although it is the work that is emphasized now, rather than the name. For all Tom Dooley's appeal, for all his fame and renown, the name neither arrests attention nor commands the immediate recognition it once did. And maybe this is as it should be, or could only be.

He was a good man, Tom Dooley, but he might have been more important historically had his life and his idealism not been bound up, however obliquely, with that colossal American fiasco: its mid-twentieth century adventure in Southeast Asia. Because of the Vietnam war, Tom Dooley couldn't win. Whether he was agent or non-agent, he stood to be the victim of that adventure, even though his life was ended before the heavy warring started. For if his idealism was not naive, it was misplaced by being invested so unquestioningly in that thing called patriotism. And if his altruism was not tainted by some secret Washington connection, then it was compromised by the fact that

** In 1970, another medical service organization was founded by Dooley friends to further his work: Tom Dooley Heritage, Inc. It has provided funds, clothing, vitamins and medicine for hospitals and orphanages in Vietnam and Laos. Tom Dooley Heritage Doctors are said to treat an average of 5,000 sick and malnourished patients each month. The organization operates out of Post Office Box 1907 at New York's Grand Central Station and is headed by Teresa E. Gallagher, a close associate of Dooley's.

he was an accessory in a dubious national scheme merely by being on the scene and "displaying the colors," if only from a jeep. Whichever way, Tom Dooley's pedestal could not remain uncracked once the story of American intrusion, subversion, complicity in the affairs of Indochinese nations began to come out. The details were too sickening and sinister for anyone's reputation to survive without tarnish. Tom Dooley could be a saint in heaven, but the devil's advocate still might have a question or two about Dooley and Southeast Asia.

This is not to say that Tom Dooley was a part of anything that was blatantly sinister in a personal sense. He wasn't in on the assassination of Ngo Dinh Diem; I'm sure that unlike some statesmen he never ticketed a Communist hospital for attack. He was, as I said, a good man—an innocent, really. But by being an innocent where he was, when he was, he very probably was dupe. Strike the qualification; he *was* dupe. It's sad, sad enough to make you want to hang down your head for Tom Dooley. But don't! He might have been a fool for patriotism, but he was no fool before God, or of his profession. That cancels out a lot of criticism.

So maybe it is no surprise after all that there actually should be a Tom Dooley canonization cause. By his own values, he led a holy and exemplary life; by anyone's definition, he arrested the world's attention and uplifted the spirits of many. Inevitably therefore there should be those who would work to keep his memory alive, enshrine it even in the galaxy of the saints.

In the mid-1960s, a movement was started seeking his canonization. It foundered, presumably because it was begun too soon after his death. Good causes, like good wine, must age some.

In early 1975, a second canonization effort was launched by Oblate Father Maynard C. Kegler, an old Dooley friend and director of a retreat house in Buffalo, Minnesota. Now articles crop up fairly regularly in the Catholic press—the Providence *Visitor, The Catholic Digest,* the *Messenger of St. Anthony*—championing the Dooley cause. Some of the material is ecstatic, making the success of the cause seem almost imminent. In point of fact the status of the cause is nowhere near so advanced as the enthusiasm of some of its proponents. Indeed it is only in the tentative stage. "We are making all *preliminary* investigations to evaluate whether or not the cause is worthy of introduction with the Sacred Congregation of Saints," Father Kegler told me in November, 1977. "It would be useless for us to introduce the cause if we thought it had no merit, and if we knew it would not be accepted. So we are now collecting data, reliable information from those who knew Tom personally, to sound out their evaluation of Tom. It will be some time yet before Father Mitri [Rev. Angelo Mitri, O.M.I., Postulator of Oblate Causes in Rome] can judge the worthiness of Tom's cause, and make the decision whether or not to present it for introduction. As you know these things take a lot of time, prayer and reflection, and good sense as well."

Good sense is Father Kegler's. Good sense is not always evident in Catholic-press articles. But that may make no difference in the long run. If Tom's "up there," and if he has the public-relations touch in heaven that he had on earth—well, he can overcome anything, including the enthusiasm of devotees. It will just take a little time—such time as is necessary to work up a few miracles or extraordinary favors, of which there are none yet chalked up to Dooley. Like, maybe, a couple of centuries. As Father Kegler has noted, "Past history shows that canonizations can take two hundred years or longer." Obviously we're going to have to wait a spell.